CW01647710

ARM
Assembly Language Programming

By Pete Cockerell

Published by
M.T.C.
• Gaddesden Place • Hemel Hempstead • Hertfordshire HP2 6EX •
ENGLAND

First Edition 1987.

Contents

1. First concepts

Like most interesting subjects, assembly language programming requires a little background knowledge before you can start to appreciate it. In this chapter, we explore these basics. If terms such as two's complement, hexadecimal, index register and byte are familiar to you, the chances are you can skip to the next chapter, or skim through this one for revision. Otherwise, most of the important concepts you will need to understand to start programming in assembler are explained below.

One prerequisite, even for the assembly language beginner, is a familiarity with some high-level language such as BASIC or Pascal. In explaining some of the important concepts, we make comparisons to similar ideas in BASIC, C or Pascal. If you don't have this fundamental requirement, you may as well stop reading now and have a bash at BASIC first.

1.1 Machine code and up...

The first question we need to answer is, of course, 'What is assembly language'. As you know, any programming language is a medium through which humans may give instructions to a computer. Languages such as BASIC, Pascal and C, which we call high-level languages, bear some relationship to English, and this enables humans to represent ideas in a fairly natural way. For example, the idea of performing an operation a number of times is expressed using the BASIC **FOR** construct:

```
FOR i=1 TO 10 : PRINT i : NEXT i
```

Although these high-level constructs enable us humans to write programs in a relatively painless way, they in fact bear little relationship to the way in which the computer performs the operations. All a computer can do is manipulate patterns of 'on' and 'off', which are usually represented by the presence or absence of an electrical signal.

To explain this seemingly unbridgable gap between electrical signals and our familiar **FOR...NEXT** loops, we use several levels of representation. At the lowest level we have our electrical signals. In a digital computer of the type we're interested in, a circuit may be at one of two levels, say 0 volts ('off') or 5 volts ('on').

Now we can't tell very easily just by looking what voltage a circuit is at, so we choose to write patterns of on/off voltages using some visual representation. The digits 0 and 1 are used. These digits are used because, in addition to neatly representing the idea of an absence or presence of a signal, 0 and 1 are the digits of the binary number system, which is central to the understanding of how a computer works. The term binary digit is usually abbreviated to *bit*. Here is a bit: 1. Here are eight bits in a row: 11011011

Machine code

Suppose we have some way of storing groups of binary digits and feeding them into the computer. On reading a particular pattern of bits, the computer will react in some way. This is absolutely deterministic; that is, every time the computer sees that pattern its response will be the same. Let's say we have a mythical computer which reads in groups of bits eight at a time, and according to the pattern of 1s and 0s in the group, performs some task. On reading this pattern, for example

    10100111

the computer might produce a voltage on a wire, and on reading the pattern

    10100110

it might switch off that voltage. The two patterns may then be regarded as instructions to the computer, the first meaning 'voltage on', the second 'voltage off'. Every time the instruction 10100111 is read, the voltage will come on, and whenever the pattern 10100110 is encountered, the computer turns the voltage off. Such patterns of bits are called the machine code of a computer; they are the codes which the raw machinery reacts to.

Assembly language and assemblers

There are 256 combinations of eight 1s and 0s, from 00000000 to 11111111, with 254 others in between. Remembering what each of these means is asking too much of a human: we are only good at remembering groups of at most six or seven items. To make the task of remembering the instructions a little easier, we resort to the next step in the progression towards the high-level instructions found in BASIC. Each machine code instruction is given a name, or *mnemonic*. Mnemonics often consist of three letters, but this is by no means obligatory. We could make up mnemonics for our two machine codes:

ON	means	10100111
OFF	means	10100110

So whenever we write **ON** in a program, we really mean 10100111, but **ON** is easier to remember. A program written using these textual names for instructions is called an assembly language program, and the set of mnemonics that is used to represent a computer's machine code is called the assembly language of that computer. Assembly language is the lowest level used by humans to program a computer; only an incurable masochist would program using pure machine code.

It is usual for machine codes to come in groups which perform similar functions. For example, whereas 10100111 might mean switch on the voltage at the signal called 'output 0', the very similar pattern 10101111 could mean switch on the signal called 'output 1'. Both instructions are '**ON**' ones, but they affect different signals. Now we could define two mnemonics, say **ON0** and **ON1**, but it is much more usual in assembly language to use the simple mnemonic **ON** and follow this with extra information saying which signal we want to switch on. For example, the assembly language instruction

```
ON      1
```

would be translated into 10101111, whereas:

```
ON      0
```

is 10100111 in machine code. The items of information which come after the mnemonic (there might be more than one) are called the *operands* of the instruction.

How does an assembly program, which is made up of textual information, get converted into the machine code for the computer? We write a program to do it, of course! Well, we don't write it. Whoever supplies the computer writes it for us. The program is called an assembler. The process of using an assembler to convert from mnemonics to machine code is called assembling. We shall have more to say about one particular assembler - which converts from ARM assembly language into ARM machine code - in Chapter Four.

Compilers and interpreters

As the subject of this book is ARM assembly language programming, we could halt the discussion of the various levels of instructing the computer here. However, for completeness we will briefly discuss the missing link between assembly language and, say, Pascal. The Pascal assignment

```
a  :=  a+12
```

looks like a simple operation to us, and so it should. However, the computer knows nothing of variables called **a** or decimal numbers such as 12. Before the computer can do what we've asked, the assignment must be translated into a suitable sequence of instructions. Such a sequence (for some mythical computer) might be:

```
LOAD   a
ADD    12
STORE  a
```

Here we see three mnemonics, **LOAD**, **ADD** and **STORE**. **LOAD** obtains the value from the place we've called **a**, **ADD** adds 12 to this loaded value, and **STORE** saves it away again. Of course, this assembly language sequence must be converted into machine code before it can be obeyed. The three mnemonics above might convert into these instructions:

```
00010011
00111100
00100011
```

Once this machine code has been programmed into the computer, it may be obeyed, and the initial assignment carried out.

To get from Pascal to the machine code, we use another program. This is called a compiler. It is similar to an assembler in that it converts from a human-readable program into something a computer can understand. There is one important difference though: whereas there is a one-to-one relationship between an assembly language instruction and the machine code it represents, there is no such relationship between a high-level language instruction such as

```
PRINT  "HELLO"
```

and the machine code a compiler produces which has the same effect. Therein lies one of the advantages of programming in assembler: you know at all times exactly what the computer is up to and have very intimate control over it. Additionally, because a compiler is only a program, the machine code it produces can rarely be as 'good' as that which a human could write.

A compiler has to produce working machine code for the infinite number of programs that can be written in the language it compiles. It is impossible to ensure that all possible high-level instructions are translated in the optimum way; faster and smaller human-written assembly language programs will always be possible. Against these advantages of using assembler must be weighed the fact that high-level languages are, by definition, easier for humans to write, read and debug (remove the errors).

The process of writing a program in a high-level language, running the compiler on it, correcting the mistakes, re-compiling it and so on is often time consuming, especially for large programs which may take several minutes (or even hours) to compile. An alternative approach is provided by another technique used to make the transition from high-level language to machine code. This technique is know as interpreting. The most popular interpreted language is BASIC.

An interpreted program is not converted from, say, BASIC text into machine code. Instead, a program (the interpreter) examines the BASIC program and decides which operations to perform to produce the desired effect. For example, to interpret the assignment

```
LET   a=a+12
```

in BASIC, the interpreter would do something like the following:

1. Look at the command **`LET`**
2. This means assignment, so look for the variable to be assigned
3. Check there's an equals sign after the **`a`**
4. If not, give a **`Missing =`** error
5. Find out where the value for **`a`** is stored
6. Evaluate the expression after the =
7. Store that value in the right place for **`a`**

Notice at step 6 we simplify things by not mentioning exactly *how* the expression after the = is evaluated. In reality, this step, called 'expression evaluation' can be quite a complex operation.

The advantage of operating directly on the BASIC text like this is that an interpreted language can be made interactive. This means that program lines can be changed and the effect seen immediately, without time-consuming recompilation; and the values of variables may be inspected and changed 'on the fly'. The drawback is that the interpreted program will run slower than an equivalent compiled one because of all the checking (for equals signs etc.) that has to occur every time a statement is executed. Interpreters are usually written in assembler for speed, but it is also possible to write one in a high-level language.

Summary

We can summarise what we have learnt in this section as follows. Computers understand (respond to) the presence or absence of voltages. We can represent these voltages on paper by sequences of 1s and 0s (bits). The set of bit sequences which cause the computer to respond in some well-defined way is called its machine code. Humans can't tell 10110111 from

10010111 very well, so we give short names, or mnemonics, to instructions. The set of mnemonics is the assembly language of the computer, and an assembler is a program to convert from this representation to the computer-readable machine code. A compiler does a similar job for high-level languages.

1.2 Computer architecture

So far we have avoided the question of how instructions are stored, how the computer communicates with the outside world, and what operations a typical computer is actually capable of performing. We will now clear up these points and introduce some more terminology.

The CPU

In the previous section, we used the word 'computer' to describe what is really only one component of a typical computer system. The part which reads instructions and carries them out (*executes* them) is called the processor, or more fully, the central processing unit (CPU). The CPU is the heart of any computer system, and in this book we are concerned with one particular type of CPU - the Acorn RISC Machine or ARM.

In most microcomputer systems, the CPU occupies a single chip (integrated circuit), housed in a plastic or ceramic package. The ARM CPU is in a square package with 84 connectors around the sides. Section 1.4 describes in some detail the major elements of the ARM CPU. In this section we are more concerned with how it connects with the rest of the system.

Computer busses

The diagram below shows how the CPU slots into the whole system:

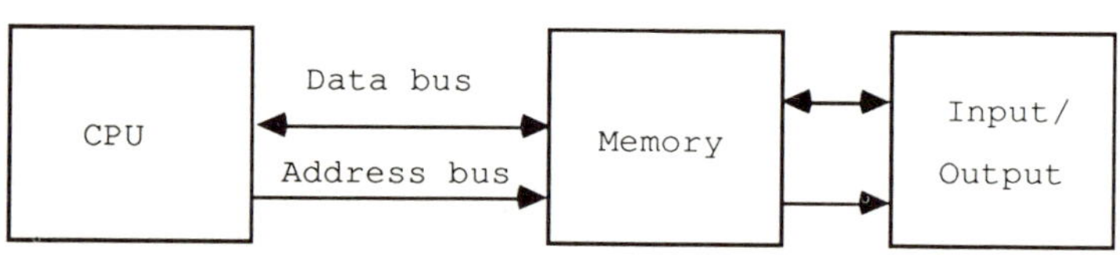

This is a much simplified diagram of a computer system, but is shows the three main components and how they are connected. The CPU has already been mentioned. Emanating from it are two busses. A bus in this context is a group of wires carrying signals. There are two of them on the diagram. The data bus is used to transfer information (data) in and out of the CPU. The address bus is produced by the CPU to tell the other devices (memory and input/output) which particular item of information is required.

Busses are said to have certain *widths*. This is just the number of signals that make up the bus. For a given processor the width of the data bus is usually fixed; typical values are 8, 16 and 32 bits. On the ARM the data bus is 32 bits wide (i.e. there are 32 separate signals for transferring data), and the ARM is called a 32-bit machine. The wider the data bus, the larger the amount of information that can be processed in one go by the CPU. Thus it is generally said that 32-bit computers are more powerful than 16-bit ones, which in turn are more powerful than 8-bit ones.

The ARM's address bus has 26 signals. The wider the address bus, the more memory the computer is capable of using. For each extra signal, the amount of memory possible is doubled. Many CPUs (particularly the eight-bit ones, found in many older home and desk-top micros) have a sixteen-bit address bus, allowing 65,536 memory cells to be addressed. The ARM's address bus has 26 signals, allowing over 1000 times as much memory.

As we said above, the ARM has 84 signals. 58 of these are used by the data and address busses; the remainder form yet another bus, not shown on the diagram. This is called the control signal bus, and groups together the signals required to perform tasks such as synchronising the flow of information between the ARM and the other devices.

Memory and I/O

The arrows at either end of the data bus imply that information may flow in and out of the computer. The two blocks from where information is received, and to where it is sent, are labelled Memory and Input/output. Memory is where programs, and all the information associated with them, are held. Earlier we talked about instructions being read by the CPU. Now we can see that they are read from the computer's memory, and pass along the data bus to the CPU. Similarly, when the CPU needs to read information to be processed, or to write results back, the data travels to and fro along the data bus.

Input/output (I/O) covers a multitude of devices. To be useful, a computer must communicate with the outside world. This could be via a screen and keyboard in a personal computer, or using temperature sensors and pumps if the computer happened to be controlling a central heating system. Whatever the details of the computer's I/O, the CPU interacts with it through the data bus. In fact, to many CPUs (the ARM being one) I/O devices 'look' like normal memory; this is called memory-mapped I/O.

The other bus on the diagram is the Address Bus. A computer's memory (and I/O) may be regarded as a collection of cells, each of which may contain n bits of information, where n is the width of the data bus. Some way must be provided to select any one of these cells individually. The function of the address bus is to provide a code which uniquely identifies the desired cell. We mentioned above that there are 256 combinations of eight bits, so an 8-bit address bus would enable us to uniquely identify 256 memory cells. In practice this is far too few, and real CPUs provide at least 16 bits of address bus: 65536 cells may be addressed using such a bus. As already mentioned the ARM has a 26-bit address bus, which allows 64 million cells (or 'locations') to be addressed.

Instructions

It should now be clearer how a CPU goes about its work. When the processor is started up (*reset*) it fetches an instruction from some fixed location. On the ARM this is the location accessed when all 26 bits of the address bus are 0. The instruction code - 32 bits of it on the ARM - is transferred from memory into the CPU. The circuitry in the CPU figures out what the instruction means (this is called *decoding* the instruction) and performs the appropriate action. Then, another instruction is fetched from the next location, decoded and executed, and so on. This sequence is the basis of all work done by the CPU. It is the fact that the fetch-decode-execute cycle may be performed so quickly that makes computers fast. The ARM, for example, can manage a peak of 8,000,000 cycles a second. Section 1.4 says more about the fetch-decode-execute cycle.

What kind of instructions does the ARM understand? On the whole they are rather simple, which is one reason why they can be performed so quickly. One group of instructions is concerned with simple arithmetic: adding two numbers and so on. Another group is used to load and store data into and out of the CPU. One particular instruction causes the ARM to abandon its usual sequential mode of fetching instructions and start from somewhere else in the memory. A large proportion of this book deals with detailed descriptions of all of the ARM instructions - in terms of their assembly language mnemonics rather than the 32-bit codes which are actually represented by the electric signals in the chips.

Summary

The ARM, in common with most other CPUs, is connected to memory and I/O devices through the data bus and address bus. Memory is used to store instructions and data. I/O is used to interface the CPU to the outside world. Instructions are fetched in a normally sequential fashion, and executed by the CPU. The ARM has a 32-bit data bus, which means it usually deals with data of this size. There are 26 address signals, enabling the ARM to address 64 million memory or I/O locations.

1.3 Bits, bytes and binary

Earlier we stated the choice of the digits 0 and 1 to represent signals was important as it tied in with the binary arithmetic system. In this section we explain what binary representation is, and how the signals appearing on the data and address busses may be interpreted as binary numbers.

All data and instructions in computers are stored as sequences of ones and zeros, as mentioned above. Each binary digit, or bit, may have one of two values, just as a decimal digit may have one of the ten values 0-9.

We group bits into lots of eight. Such a group is called a byte, and each bit in the byte represents a particular value. To understand this, consider what the decimal number 3456 means:

10^3	10^2	10^1	10^0	
Thousands	Hundreds	Tens	Units	
3	4	5	6	
3000 +	400 +	50 +	6 =	3456

Each digit position represents a power of ten. The rightmost one gives the number of units (ten to the zeroth power), then the tens (ten to the one) and so on. Each column's significance is ten times greater than the one on its right. We can write numbers as big as we like by using enough digits.

Now look at the binary number 1101:

2^3	2^2	2^1	2^0	
Eights	Fours	Twos	Units	
1	1	0	1	
8 +	4 +	0 +	1 =	13

Once again the rightmost digit represents units. The next digit represents twos (two to the one) and so on. Each column's significance is twice as great as the one on its right, and we can represent any number by using enough bits.

The way in which a sequence of bits is interpreted depends on the context in which it is used. For example, in section 1.1 we had a mythical computer which used eight-bit instructions. Upon fetching the byte 10100111 this computer caused a signal to come on. In another context, the binary number 10100111 might be one of two values which the computer is adding together. Here it is used to represent a quantity:

$$1*2^7 + 0*2^6 + 1*2^5 + 0*2^4 + 0*2^3 + 1*2^2 + 1*2^1 + 1*2^0 =$$

$$128 + 32 + 4 + 2 + 1 = 167$$

If we want to specify a particular bit in a number, we refer to it by the power of two which it represents. For example, the rightmost bit represents two to the zero, and so is called bit zero. This is also called the least significant bit (LSB), as it represents the smallest magnitude. Next to the LSB is bit 1, then bit 2, and so on. The highest bit of a N-bit number will be bit N-1, and naturally enough, this is called the most significant bit - MSB.

As mentioned above, bits are usually grouped into eight-bit bytes. A byte can therefore represent numbers in the range 00000000 to 11111111 in binary, or 0 to 128+64+32+16+8+4+2+1 = 255 in decimal. (We shall see how negative numbers are represented below.)

Where larger numbers are required, several bytes may be used to increase the range. For example, two bytes can represent 65536 different values and four-byte (32-bit) numbers have over 4,000,000,000 values.

As the ARM operates on 32-bit numbers, it can quite easily deal with numbers of the magnitude just mentioned. However, as we will see below, byte-sized quantities are also very useful, so the ARM can deal with single bytes too.

In addition to small integers, bytes are used to represent characters. Characters that you type at the keyboard or see on the screen are given codes. For example, the upper-case letter A is given the code 65. Thus a byte which has value 65 could be said to represent the letter A. Given that codes in the range 0-255 are available, we can represent one of 256 different characters in a byte.

In the environment under which you will probably be using the ARM, 223 of the possible codes are used to represent characters you can see on the screen. 95 of these are the usual symbols you see on the keyboard, e.g. the letters, digits and punctuation characters. Another 128 are special characters, e.g. accented letters and maths symbols. The remaining 33 are not used to represent printed characters, but have special meanings.

Binary arithmetic

Just as we can perform various operations such as addition and subtraction on decimal numbers, we can do arithmetic on binary numbers. In fact, designing circuits to perform, for example, binary addition is much easier than designing those to operate on 'decimal' signals (where we would have ten voltage levels instead of two), and this is one of the main reasons for using binary.

The rules for adding two decimal digits are:

```
0 + 0 = 0
0 + 1 = 1
1 + 0 = 1
1 + 1 = 0  carry 1
```

To add the two four-bit numbers 0101 and 1001 (i.e. 5+9) we would start from the right and add corresponding digits. If a carry is generated (i.e. when adding 1 and 1), it is added to the next digit on the right. For example:

```
      0 1 0 1
+     1 0 0 1
_________1_
      1 1 1 0

= 8 + 4 + 2 = 14
```

Binary subtraction is defined in a similar way:

```
0 - 0 = 0
0 - 1 = 1 borrow 1
1 - 0 = 1
1 - 1 = 0
```

An example is 1001 - 0101 (9-5 in decimal):

```
      1 0 0 1
-     0 1 0 1
      _1____
      0 1 0 0

      = 4
```

So far we have only talked about positive numbers. We obviously need to be able to represent negative quantities too. One way is to use one bit (usually the MSB) to represent the sign - 0 for positive and 1 for negative. This is analogous to using a + or - sign when writing decimal numbers. Unfortunately it has some drawbacks when used with binary arithmetic, so isn't very common.

The most common way of representing a negative number is to use 'two's complement' notation. We obtain the representation for a number -n simply by performing the subtraction 0 - n. For example, to obtain the two's complement notation for -4 in a four-bit number system, we would do:

```
    0 0 0 0
-   0 1 0 0
   _1_ _ _ _
    1 1 0 0
```

So -4 in a four-bit two's complement notation is 1100. But wait a moment! Surely 1100 is twelve? Well, yes and no. If we are using the four bits to represent an unsigned (i.e. positive) number, then yes, 1100 is twelve in decimal. If we are using two's complement notation, then half of the possible combinations (those with MSB = 1) must be used to represent the negative half of the number range. The table below compares the sixteen possible four bit numbers in unsigned and two's complement interpretation:

Binary	**Unsigned**	**Two's complement**
0000	0	0
0001	1	1
0010	2	2
0011	3	3
0100	4	4
0101	5	5
0110	6	6
0111	7	7
1000	8	-8
1001	9	-7
1010	10	-6
1011	11	-5
1100	12	-4
1101	13	-3
1110	14	-2
1111	15	-1

One of the advantages of two's complement is that arithmetic works just as well for negative numbers as it does for positive ones. For example, to add 6 and -3, we would use:

```
       0 1 1 0
+      1 1 0 1
      _1_ _ _ _
       0 0 1 1   = 3
```

Notice that when the two MSBs were added, a carry resulted, which was ignored in the final answer. When we perform arithmetic on the computer, we can tell whether this happens and take the appropriate action.

Some final notes about two's complement. The width of the number is important. For example, although 1100 represents -4 in a four-bit system, 01100 is +14 is a five-bit system. -4 would be 11100 as a five bit number. On the ARM, as operations are on 32-bit numbers, the two's complement range is approximately -2,000,000,000 to +2,000,000,000.

The number -1 is always 'all ones', i.e. 1111 in a four-bit system, 11111111 in eight bits etc.

To find the negative version of a number n, invert all of its bits (i.e. make all the 1s into 0s and vice versa) and add 1. For example, to find -10 in an eight-bit two's complement form:

10	is	00001010
inverted	is	11110101
plus 1	is	11110110

Hexadecimal

It is boring to have to write numbers in binary as they get so long and hard to remember. Decimal could be used, but this tends to hide the significance of individual bits in a number. For example, 110110 and 100110 look as though they are connected in binary, having only one different bit, but their decimal equivalents 54 and 38 don't look at all related.

To get around this problem, we often call on the services of yet another number base, 16 or hexadecimal. The theory is just the same as with binary and decimal, with each hexadecimal digit having one of sixteen different values. We run out of normal digits at 9, so the letters A-F are used to represent the values between 11 and 15 (in decimal). The table below shows the first sixteen numbers in all three bases:

Decimal	Binary	Hexadecimal
0	0000	00
1	0001	01
2	0010	02
3	0011	03
4	0100	04
5	0101	05
6	0110	06
7	0111	07
8	1000	08
9	1001	09
10	1010	0A
11	1011	0B
12	1100	0C
13	1101	0D
14	1110	0E
15	1111	0F

Hexadecimal (or hex, as it is usually abbreviated) numbers are preceded by an ampersand & in this book to distinguish them from decimal numbers. For example, the hex number &D9F is $13*16^2 + 9*16 + 15$ or 3487.

The good thing about hex is that it is very easy to convert between hex and binary representation. Each hexadecimal digit is formed from four binary digits grouped from the left. For example:

11010110 = 1101 0110 = D 6 = &D6
11110110 = 1001 0110 = F 6 = &F6

The examples show that a small change in the binary version of a number produces a small change in the hexadecimal representation.

The ranges of numbers that can be held in various byte multiples are also easy to represent in hex. A single byte holds a number in the range &00 to &FF, two bytes in the range &0000 to &FFFF and four bytes in the range &00000000 to &FFFFFFFF.

As with binary, whether a given hex number represents a negative quantity is a matter of interpretation. For example, the byte &FE may represent 254 or -2, depending on how we wish to interpret it.

Large numbers

We often refer to large quantities. To save having to type, for example 65536, too frequently, we use a couple of useful abbreviations. The letter K after a number means 'Kilo' or 'times 1024'. (Note this Kilo is slightly larger than the kilo (1000) used in kilogramme etc.) 1024 is two to the power ten and is a convenient unit when discussing, say, memory capacities. For example, one might say 'The BBC Micro Model B has 32K bytes of RAM,' meaning 32*1024 or 32768 bytes.

For even larger numbers, mega (abbr. M) is used to represent 1024*1024 or just over one million. An example is 'This computer has 1M byte of RAM.'

Memory and addresses

The memory of the ARM is organised as bytes. Each byte has its own address, starting from 0. The theoretical upper limit on the number of bytes the ARM can access is determined by the width of the address bus. This is 26 bits, so the highest address is (deep breath) 11111111111111111111111111 or &3FFFFFF or 67,108,863. This enables the ARM to access 64M bytes of memory. In practice, a typical system will have one or four megabytes, still a very reasonable amount.

The ARM is referred to as a 32-bit micro. This means that it deals with data in 32-bit or four-byte units. Each such unit is called a word (and 32-bits is the word-length of the ARM). Memory is organised as words, but can be accessed either as words or bytes. The ARM is a byte-addressable machine, because every single byte in memory has its own address, in the sequence 0, 1, 2 , and so on.

When complete words are accessed (e.g. when loading an instruction), the ARM requires a word-aligned address, that is, one which is a multiple of four bytes. So the first complete word is at address 0, the second at address 4, and so on.

The way in which each word is used depends entirely on the whim of the programmer. For example, a given word could be used to hold an instruction, four characters, or a single 32-bit number, or 32 one-bit numbers. It may even be used to store the address of another word. The ARM does not put any interpretation on the contents of memory, only the programmer does.

When multiple bytes are used to store large numbers, there are two ways in which the bytes may be organised. The (slightly) more common way - used by the ARM - is to store the bytes in order of increasing significance. For example, a 32-bit number stored at addresses 8..11 will have bits 0..7 at address 8, bits 8..15 at address 9, bits 16..23 at address 10, and bits 24..31 at address 11.

If two consecutive words are used to store a 64-bit number, the first word would contain bits 0..31 and the second word bits 32..63.

There are two main types of memory. The programs you will write and the data associated with them are stored in read/write memory. As its name implies, this may be written to (i.e. altered) or read from. The common abbreviation for read/write memory is RAM. This comes from the somewhat misleading term Random Access Memory. All memory used by ARMs is Random Access, whether it is read/write or not, but RAM is universally accepted to mean read/write.

RAM is generally volatile, that is, its contents are forgotten when the power is removed. Most machines provide a small amount of non-volatile memory (powered by a rechargeable battery when the mains is switched off) to store information which is only changed very rarely, e.g. preferences about the keyboard auto-repeat rate.

The other type of memory is ROM - Read-only memory. This is used to store instructions and data which must not be erased, even when the power is removed. For example the program which is obeyed when the ARM is first turned on is held in ROM.

Summary

We have seen that computers use the binary number system due to the 'two-level' nature of the circuits from which they are constructed. Binary arithmetic is simple to implement in chips. To make life easier for humans we use hexadecimal notation to write down numbers such as addresses which would contain many bits, and assembly language to avoid having to remember the binary instruction codes.

The memory organisation of the ARM consists of 16 megawords, each of which contains four individually addressable bytes.

1.4 Inside the CPU

In this section we delve into the CPU, which has been presented only as a black box so far. We know already that the CPU presents two busses to the outside world. The data bus is used to transfer data and instructions between the CPU and memory or I/O. The address contains the address of the current location being accessed.

There are many other signals emanating from CPU. Examples of such signals on the ARM are r/w which tells the outside world whether the CPU is reading or writing data; b/w which indicates whether a data transfer is to operate on just one byte or a whole word; and two signals which indicate which of four possible 'modes' the ARM is in.

If we could examine the circuitry of the processor we would see thousands of transistors, connected to form common logic circuits. These go by names such as NAND gate, flip-flop, barrel shifter and arithmetic-logic unit (ALU).

Luckily for us programmers, the signals and components mentioned in the two previous paragraphs are of very little interest. What interests us is the way all of these combine to form an abstract model whose behaviour we can control by writing programs. This is called the 'programmers' model', and it describes the processor in terms of what appears to the programmer, rather than the circuits used to implement it.

The next chapter describes in detail the programmers' model of the ARM. In this section, we will complete our simplified look at computer architecture by outlining the purpose of the main blocks in the CPU. As mentioned above, a knowledge of these blocks isn't vital to write programs in assembly language. However, some of the terms do crop up later, so there's no harm in learning about them.

The instruction cycle

We have already mentioned the fetch-decode-execute cycle which the CPU performs continuously. Here it is in more detail, starting from when the CPU is reset.

Inside the CPU is a 24-bit store that acts as a counter. On reset, it is set to &000000. The counter holds the address of the next instruction to be fetched. It is called the program counter (PC). When the processor is ready to read the next instruction from memory, it places the contents of the PC on to the address bus. In particular, the PC is placed on bits 2..25 of the address bus. Bits 0 and 1 are always 0 when the CPU fetches an instruction, as instructions are always on word addresses, i.e. multiples of four bytes.

The CPU also outputs signals telling the memory that this is a read operation, and that it requires a whole word (as opposed to a single byte). The memory system responds to these signals by placing the contents of the addressed cell on to the data bus, where it can be read by the processor. Remember that the data bus is 32 bits wide, so an instruction can be read in one read operation.

From the data bus, the instruction is transferred into the first stage of a three-stage storage area inside the CPU. This is called the pipeline, and at any time it can hold three instructions: the one just fetched, the one being decoded, and the one being executed. After an instruction has finished executing, the pipeline is shifted up one place, so the just-decoded instruction starts to be executed, the previously fetched instruction starts to be decoded, and the next instruction is fetched from memory.

Decoding the instruction involves deciding exactly what needs to be done, and preparing parts of the CPU for this. For example, if the instruction is an addition, the two numbers to be added will be obtained.

When an instruction reaches the execute stage of the pipeline, the appropriate actions take place, a subtraction for example, and the next instruction, which has already been decoded, is executed. Also, the PC is incremented to allow the next instruction to be fetched.

In some circumstances, it is not possible to execute the next pipelined instruction because of the effect of the last one. Some instructions explicitly alter the value of the PC, causing the program to jump (like a GOTO in BASIC). When this occurs, the pre-fetched instruction is not the correct one to execute, and the pipeline has to be flushed (emptied), and the fetch-decode cycle started from the new location. Flushing the pipeline tends to slow down execution (because the fetch, decode and execute cycles no longer all happen at the same time) so the ARM provides ways of avoiding many of the jumps.

The ALU and barrel shifter

Many ARM instructions make use of these two very important parts of the CPU. There is a whole class of instructions, called the data manipulation group, which use these units. The arithmetic-logic unit performs operations such as addition, subtraction and comparison. These are the arithmetic operations. Logical operations include AND, EOR and OR, which are described in the next chapter.

The ALU can be regarded as a black-box which takes two 32-bit numbers as input, and produces a 32-bit result. The instruction decode circuitry tells the ALU which of its repertoire of operations to perform by examining the instruction. It also works out where to find the two input numbers - the operands - and where to put the result from the instruction.

The barrel shifter has two inputs - a 32-bit word to be shifted and a count - and one output - another 32-bit word. As its name implies, the barrel shifter obtains its output by shifting the bits of the operand in some way. There are several flavours of shift: which direction the bits are shifted in, whether the bits coming out of one end re-appear in the other end etc. The varieties of shift operation on the ARM are described in the next chapter.

The important property of the barrel shifter is that no matter what type of shift it does, and by how many bits, it always takes only one 'tick' of the CPU's master clock to do it. This is much better than many 16 and 32-bit processors, which take a time proportional to the number of shifts required.

Registers

When we talked about data being transferred from memory to the CPU, we didn't mention exactly where in the CPU the data went. An important part of the CPU is the register bank. In fact, from the programmer's point of view, the registers are more important than other components such as the ALU, as they are what he actually 'sees' when writing programs.

A register is a word of storage, like a memory location. On the ARM, all registers are one word long, i.e. 32 bits. There are several important differences between memory and registers. Firstly, registers are not 'memory mapped', that is they don't have 26-bit addresses like the rest of storage and I/O on the ARM.

Because registers are on the CPU chip rather than part of an external memory system, the CPU can access their contents very quickly. In fact, almost all operations on the ARM involve the use of registers. For example, the ADD instruction adds two 32-bit numbers to produce a 32-bit result. Both of the numbers to be added, and the destination of the result, are specified as ARM registers. Many CPUs also have instructions to, for example, add a number stored in memory to a register. This is not the case on the ARM, and the only register-memory operations are load and store ones.

The third difference is that there are far fewer registers than memory locations. As we stated earlier, the ARM can address up to 64M bytes (16M words) of external memory. Internally, there are only 16 registers visible at once. These are referred to in programs as R0 to 15. A couple of the registers are sometimes given special names; for example R15 is also called PC, because it holds the program counter value that we metioned above.

As we shall see in the next chapter, you can generally use any of the registers to hold operands and results, there being no distinction for example between R0 and R12. This availability of a large (compared to many CPUs) number of rapidly accessible registers contributes to the ARM's reputation as a fast processor.

1.5 A small program

This chapter would be irredeemably tedious if we didn't include at least one example of an assembly language program. Although we haven't actually met the ARM's set of instructions yet, you should be able to make some sense of the simple program below.

On the left is a listing of a simple BASIC **FOR** loop which prints 20 stars on the screen. On the right is the ARM assembly language program which performs the same task.

BASIC

```
10 i=1
20 PRINT "*";
30 i=i+1
40 IF i<=20 THEN 20
```

ARM Assembly Language

```
     MOV R0,#1          ;Initialise count
.loopSWI writeI+"*"    ;Print a *
     ADD R0,R0,#1       ;Increment count
     CMP R0,#20         ;Compare with limit
     BLE loop           ;Repeat if required
```

Even if this is the first assembly language program you have seen, most of the ARM instructions should be self-explanatory. The word **loop** marks the place in the program which is used by the **BLE** (branch if less than or equal to) instruction. It is called a label, and fulfils a similar function to the line number in a BASIC instruction such as **GOTO 20**.

One thing you will notice about the ARM program is that it is a line longer than the BASIC one. This is because in general, a single ARM instruction does less processing than a BASIC one. For example, the BASIC **IF** statement performs the function of the two ARM instructions **CMP** and **BLE**. Almost invariably, a program written in assembler will occupy more lines than an equivalent one written in BASIC or some other high-level language, usually by a much bigger ratio than the one illustrated.

However, when assembled, the ARM program above will occupy five words (one per instruction) or 20 bytes. The BASIC program, as shown, takes 50 bytes, so the size of the assembly language program (the 'source') can be misleading. Furthermore, a compiled language version of the program, for example, one in Pascal:

```
for i := 1 to 20 do
    write('*');
```

occupies even fewer source lines, but when compiled into ARM machine code will use many more than 5 instructions - the exact number depending on how good the compiler is.

1.6 Summary of chapter 1

For the reader new to assembly language programming, this chapter has introduced many concepts, some of them difficult to grasp on the first reading. We have seen how computers - or the CPU in particular - reads instructions from memory and executes then. The instructions are simply patterns of 1s and 0s, which are manifestly difficult for humans to deal with efficiently. Thus we have several levels of representation, each one being further from what the CPU sees and closer to our ideal programming language, which would be an unambiguous version of English.

The lowest level of representation that humans use, and the subject of this book, is assembly language. In this language, each processor instruction is given a name, or mnemonic, which is easier to remember than a sequence of binary digits. An assembly program is a list of mnemonic instructions, plus some other items such as labels and operands. The program is converted into CPU-processable binary form by a program called an assembler. Unlike high-level languages, there is a one-to-one correspondence between assembly instructions and binary instructions.

We learned about binary representation of numbers, both signed and unsigned, and saw how simple arithmetic operations such as addition and subtraction may be performed on them.

Next, we looked inside the CPU to better understand what goes on when an instruction is fetched from memory and executed. Major components of the CPU such as the ALU and barrel shifter were mentioned. A knowledge of these is not vital for programming in assembler, but as the terms crop up in the detailed description of the ARM's instruction set, it is useful to know them.

Finally, we presented a very small assembly language program to compare and contrast it with a functionally equivalent program written in BASIC.

2. Inside the ARM

In the previous chapter, we started by considering instructions executed by a mythical processor with mnemonics like **ON** and **OFF**. Then we went on to describe some of the features of an actual processor - the ARM. This chapter looks in much more detail at the ARM, including the programmer's model and its instruction types. We'll start by listing some important attributes of the CPU:

Word size

The ARM's word length is 4 bytes. That is, it's a 32-bit micro and is most at home when dealing with units of data of that length. However, the ability to process individual bytes efficiently is important - as character information is byte oriented - so the ARM has provision for dealing with these smaller units too.

Memory

When addressing memory, ARM uses a 26-bit address value. This allows for 2^{26} or 64M bytes of memory to be accessed. Although individual bytes may be transferred between the processor and memory, ARM is really word-based. All word-sized transfers must have the operands in memory residing on word-boundaries. This means the instruction addresses have to be multiples of four.

I/O

Input and output devices are memory mapped. There is no concept of a separate I/O address space. Peripheral chips are read and written as if they were areas of memory. This means that in practical ARM systems, the memory map is divided into three areas: RAM, ROM, and input/output devices (probably in decreasing order of size).

Registers

The register set, or programmer's model, of the ARM could not really be any simpler. Many popular processors have a host of dedicated (or special-purpose) registers of varying sizes which may only be used with certain instructions or in particular circumstances. ARM has sixteen 32-bit registers which may be used without restriction in any instruction. There is very little dedication - only one of the registers being permanently tied up by the processor.

Instructions

As the whole philosophy of the ARM is based on 'fast and simple', we would expect the instruction set to reflect this, and indeed it does. A small, easily remembered set of instruction types is available. This does not imply a lack of power, though. Firstly, instructions execute very quickly, and secondly, most have useful extras which add to their utility without detracting from the ease of use.

2.1 Memory and addressing

The lowest address that ARM can use is that obtained by placing 0s on all of the 26 address lines - address &0000000. The highest possible address is obtained by placing 1s on the 26 address signals, giving address &3FFFFFF. All possible combinations between these two extremes are available, allowing a total of 64M bytes to be addressed. Of course, it is very unlikely that this much memory will actually be fitted in current machines, even with the ever-increasing capacities of RAM and ROM chips. One or four megabytes of RAM is a reasonable amount to expect using today's technology.

Why allow such a large address range then? There are several good reasons. Firstly, throughout the history of computers, designers have under-estimated how much memory programmers (or rather their programs) can actually use. A good maxim is 'programs will always grow to fill the space available. And then some.' In the brief history of microprocessors, the addressing range of CPUs has grown from 256 single bytes to 4 billion bytes (i.e. 4,000,000,000 bytes) for some 32-bit micros. As the price of memory continues to fall, we can expect 16M and even 32M byte RAM capacities to become available fairly cheaply.

Another reason for providing a large address space is to allow the possibility of using virtual memory. Virtual memory is a technique whereby the fast but relatively expensive semiconductor RAM is supplemented by slower but larger capacity magnetic storage, e.g. a Winchester disc. For example, we might allocate 16M bytes of a Winchester disc to act as memory for the computer. The available RAM is used to 'buffer' as much of this as possible, say 512K bytes, making it rapidly accessible. When the need arises to access data which is not currently in RAM, we load it in from the Winchester.

Virtual memory is an important topic, but a detailed discussion of it is outside the scope of this book. We do mention some basic virtual memory techniques when talking about the memory controller chip in Chapter Seven.

The diagram below illustrates how the ARM addresses memory words and bytes.

```
bit  31.........................bit 0
```

Address 0	byte 3	byte 2	byte 1	byte 0
Address 4	byte 7	byte 6	byte 5	byte 4
Address 8	byte 11	byte 10	byte 9	byte 8
Address 12	byte 15	byte 14	byte 13	byte 12

The addresses shown down the left hand side are word addresses, and increase in steps of four. Word addresses always have their least two significant bits set to zero and the other 24 bits determine which word is required. Whenever the ARM fetches an instruction from memory, a word address is used. Additionally, when a word-size operand is transferred from the ARM to memory, or vice versa, a word address is used.

When byte-sized operands are accessed, all 26 address lines are used, the least significant two bits specifying which byte within the word is required. There is a signal from the ARM chip which indicates whether the current transfer is a word or byte-sized one. This signal is used by the memory system to enable the appropriate memory chips. We will have more to say about addressing in the section on data transfer instructions.

The first few words of ARM memory have special significance. When certain events occur, e.g. the ARM is reset or an illegal instruction is encountered, the processor automatically jumps to one of these first few locations. The instructions there perform the necessary actions to deal with the event. Other than this, all ARM memory was created equal and its use is determined solely by the designer of the system.

For the rest of this section, we give brief details of the use of another chip in the ARM family called the MEMC. This information is not vital to most programmers, and may be skipped on the first reading.

A topic which is related to virtual memory mentioned above, and which unlike that, is within the scope of this book, is the relationship between 'physical' and 'logical' memory in ARM systems. Many ARM-based machines use a device called the Memory Controller - MEMC - which is part of the same family of devices as the ARM CPU. (Other members are the Video Controller and I/O Controller, called VIDC and IOC respectively.)

When an ARM-based system uses MEMC, its memory map is divided into three main areas. The bottom half - 32M bytes - is called logical RAM, and is the memory that most programs 'see' when they are executing. The next 16M bytes is allocated to physical RAM. This area is only visible to system programs which use the CPU in a special mode called *supervisor mode.* Finally, the top 16M bytes is occupied by ROM and I/O devices.

The logical and physical RAM is actually the same thing, and the data is stored in the same RAM chips. However, whereas physical RAM occupies a contiguous area from address 32M to 32M+(memory size)-1, logical RAM may be scattered anywhere in the bottom 32M bytes. The physical RAM is divided into 128 'pages'. The size of a page depends on how much RAM the machine has. For example, in a 1M byte machine, a page is 8K bytes; in a 4M byte machine (the maximum that the current MEMC chip can handle) it is 32K bytes.

A table in MEMC is programmed to control where each physical page appears in the logical memory map. For example, in a particular system it might be convenient to have the screen memory at the very top of the 32M byte logical memory area. Say the page size is 8K bytes and 32K is required for the screen. The MEMC would be programmed so that four pages of physical RAM appear at the top 32K bytes of the logical address space. These four pages would be accessible to supervisor mode programs at both this location and in the appropriate place in the physical memory map, and to non-supervisor programs at just the logical memory map position.

When a program accesses the logical memory, the MEMC looks up where corresponding physical RAM is and passes that address on to the RAM chips. You could imagine the address bus passing through the MEMC on its way to the memory, and being translated on the way. This translation is totally transparent to the programmer. If a program tries to access a logical memory address for which there is no corresponding physical RAM (remember only at most 4M bytes of the possible 32M can be occupied), a signal called 'data abort' is activated on the CPU. This enables attempts to access 'illegal' locations to be dealt with.

As the 4M byte limit only applies to the current MEMC chip, there is no reason why a later device shouldn't be able to access a much larger area of physical memory.

Because of the translation performed by MEMC, the logical addresses used to access RAM may be anywhere in the memory map. Looked at in another way, this means that a 1M byte machine will not necessarily appear to have all of this RAM at the bottom of the memory map; it might be scattered into different areas. For example, one 'chunk' of memory might be used for the screen and mapped onto a high address, whereas another region, used for application programs say, might start at a low address such as &8000.

Usually, the presence of MEMC in a system is if no consequence to a program, but it helps to explain how the memory map of an ARM-based computer appears as it does.

2.2 Programmer's model

This section describes the way in which the ARM presents itself to the programmer. The term 'model' is employed because although it describes what the programmer sees when programming the ARM, the internal representation may be very different. So long as programs behave as expected from the description given, these internal details are unimportant.

Occasionally however, a particular feature of the processor's operation may be better understood if you know what the ARM is getting up to internally. These situations are explained as they arise in the descriptions presented below.

As mentioned above, ARM has a particularly simple register organisation, which benefits both human programmers and compilers, which also need to generate ARM programs. Humans are well served because our feeble brains don't have to cope with such questions as 'can I use the X register as an operand with the ADD instruction?' These crop up quite frequently when programming in assembler on certain micros, making coding a tiresome task.

There are sixteen user registers. They are all 32-bits wide. Only two are dedicate; the others are general purpose and are used to store operands, results and pointers to memory. Of the two dedicated registers, only one of these is permanently used for a special purpose (it is the PC). Sixteen is quite a large number of registers to provide, some micros managing with only one general purpose register. These are called accumulator-based processors, and the 6502 is an example of such a chip.

All of the ARM's registers are general purpose. This means that wherever an instruction needs a register to be specified as an operand, any one of them may be used. This gives the programmer great freedom in deciding which registers to use for which purpose.

The motivation for providing a generous register set stems from the way in which the ARM performs most of its operations. All data manipulation instructions use registers. That is, if you want to add two 32-bit numbers, both of the numbers must be in registers, and the result is stored in a third register. It is not possible to add a number in memory to a register, or vice versa. In fact, the only time the ARM accesses memory is to fetch instructions and when executing one of the few register-to-memory transfer instructions.

So, given that most processing is restricted to using the fast internal registers, it is only fair that a reasonable number of them is provided. Studies by computer scientists have shown that eight general-purpose registers is sufficient for most types of program, so 16 should be plenty.

When designing the ARM, Acorn may well have been tempted to include even more registers, say 32, using the 'too much is never enough' maxim mentioned above. However, it is important to remember that if an instruction is to allow any register as an operand, the register number has to be encoded in the instruction. 16 registers need four bits of encoding; 32 registers would need five. Thus by increasing the number of registers, they would have decreased the number of bits available to encode other information in the instructions.

Such trade-offs are common in processor design, and the utility of the design depends on whether the decisions have been made wisely. On the whole, Acorn seems to have hit the right balance with the ARM.

There is an illustration of the programmer's model overleaf.

In the diagram, 'undedicated' means that the hardware imposes no particular use for the register. 'Dedicated' means that the ARM uses the register for a particular function - R15 is the PC. 'Semi-dedicated' implies that occasionally the hardware might use the register for some function (for storing addresses), but at other times it is undedicated. 'General purpose' indicates that if an instruction requires a register as an operand, any register may be specified.

As R0-R13 are undedicated, general purpose registers, nothing more needs to be said about them at this stage.

R0	Undedicated, general purpose
R1	Undedicated, general purpose
R2	Undedicated, general purpose
R3	Undedicated, general purpose
R4	Undedicated, general purpose
R5	Undedicated, general purpose
R6	Undedicated, general purpose
R7	Undedicated, general purpose
R8	Undedicated, general purpose
R9	Undedicated, general purpose
R10	Undedicated, general purpose
R11	Undedicated, general purpose
R12	Undedicated, general purpose
R13	Undedicated, general purpose
R14	Semi-dedicated, general purpose (link)
R15	Dedicated, general purpose (PC)

Special registers

Being slightly different from the rest, R14 and R15 are more interesting, especially R15. This is the only register which you cannot use in the same way as the rest to hold operands and results. The reason is that the ARM uses it to store the program counter and status register. These two components of R15 are explained below.

Register 14 is usually free to hold any value the user wishes. However, one instruction, 'branch with link', uses R14 to keep a copy of the PC. The next chapter describes branch with link, along with the rest of the instruction set, and this use of R14 is explained in more detail there.

The program counter

R15 is split into two parts. This is illustrated below:

31	30	29	28	27	26	25 ... 2	1	0
N	Z	C	V	I	F	Program counter	S1	S0

Bits 2 to 25 are the program counter (PC). That is, they hold the word address of the next instruction to be fetched. There are only 24 bits (as opposed to the full 26) because instructions are defined to reside on word boundaries. Thus the two lowest bits of an instruction's address are always zero, and there is no need to store them. When R15 is used to place the address of the next instruction on the address bus, bits 0 and 1 of the bus are automatically set to zero.

When the ARM is reset, the program counter is set to zero, and instructions are fetched starting from that location. Normally, the program counter is incremented after every instruction is fetched, so that a program is executed in sequence. However, some instructions alter the value of the PC, causing non-consecutive instructions to be fetched. This is how **IF...THEN...ELSE** and **REPEAT...UNTIL** type constructs are programmed in machine code.

Some signals connected to the ARM chip also affect the PC when they are activated. Reset is one such signal, and as mentioned above it causes the PC to jump to location zero. Others are IRQ and FIQ, which are mentioned below, and memory abort.

Status register

The remaining bits of R15, bits 0, 1 and 26-31, form an eight-bit status register. This contains information about the state of the processor. There are two types of status information: result status and system status. The former refers to the outcome of previous operations, for example, whether a carry was generated by an addition operation. The latter refers to the four operating modes in which the ARM may be set, and whether certain events are allowed to interrupt its processing.

Here is the layout of the status register portion of R15:

	bit 31	N	Negative result flag
Result	bit 30	Z	Zero result flag
Status	bit 29	C	Carry flag
	bit 28	V	Overflowed result flag
	bit 27	IRQ	Interrupt disable flag
System	bit 26	FIQ	Fast interrupt disable flag
Status	bit 0	S0	Processor mode 0
	bit 1	S1	Processor mode 1

The result status flags are affected by the register-to-register data operations. The exact way in which these instructions change the flags is described along with the instructions. No other instructions affect the flags, unless they are loaded explicitly (along with the rest of R15) from memory.

As each flag is stored in one bit, it has two possible states. If a flag bit has the value 1, it is said to be true, or set. If it has the value 0, the flag is false or cleared. For example, if bits 31 to 28 of R15 were 1100, the N and Z flags would be set, and V and C would be cleared.

All instructions may execute conditionally on the result flags. That is to say, a given instruction may be executed only if a given combination of flags exists, otherwise the instruction is ignored. Additionally, an instruction may be unconditional, so that it executes regardless of the state of the flags.

The processor mode flags hold a two-bit number. The state of these two bits determine the 'mode' in which the ARM executes, as follows:

s1 s0	**Mode**
0 0	User
0 1	FIQ or fast interrupt
1 0	IRQ or interrupt
1 1	SVC or supervisor

The greater part of this book is concerned only with user mode. The other modes are 'system' modes which are only required by programs which will have generally already been written on the machine you are using. Briefly, supervisor mode is entered when the ARM is reset or certain types of error occur. IRQ and FIQ modes are entered under the interrupt conditions described below.

In non-user modes, the ARM looks and behaves in a very similar way to user mode (which we have been describing). The main difference is that certain registers (e.g. R13 and R14 in supervisor mode) are replaced by 'private copies' available only in that mode. These are called R13_SVC and R14_SVC. In user mode, the supervisor mode's versions of R13 and R14 are not visible, and vice versa. In addition, S0 and S1 may not be altered in user mode, but may be in other modes. In IRQ mode, the extra registers are R13_IRQ and R14_IRQ; in FIQ mode there are seven of them - R8_FIQ to R14_FIQ.

Non-user modes are used by 'privileged' programs which may have access to hardware which the user is not allowed to touch. This is possible because a signal from the ARM reflects the state of S0 and S1 so external hardware may determine if the processor is in a user mode or not.

Finally, the status bits FIQ and IRQ are used to enable or disable the two interrupts provided by the processor. An interrupt is a signal to the chip which, when activated, causes the ARM to suspend its current action (having finished the current instruction) and set the program counter to a pre-determined value. Hardware such as disc drives use interrupts to ask for attention when they require servicing.

The ARM provides two interrupts. The IRQ (which stands for interrupt request) signal will cause the program to be suspended only if the IRQ bit in the status register is cleared. If that bit is set, the interrupt will be ignored by the processor until it is clear. The FIQ (fast interrupt) works similarly, except that the FIQ bit enables/disables it. If a FIQ interrupt is activated, the IRQ bit is set automatically, disabling any IRQ signal. The reverse is not true however, and a FIQ interrupt may be processed while an IRQ is active.

As mentioned above, the supervisor, FIQ and IRQ modes are rarely of interest to programmers other than those writing 'systems' software, and the system status bits of R15 may generally be ignored. Chapter Seven covers the differences in programming the ARM in the non-user modes.

2.3 The instructions set

To complement the regular architecture of the programmer's model, the ARM has a well-organised, uniform instruction set. In this section we give an overview of the instruction types, and defer detailed descriptions until the next chapter.

General properties

There are certain attributes that all instructions have in common. All instructions are 32-bits long (i.e. they occupy one word) and must lie on word boundaries. We have already seen that the address held in the program counter is a word address, and the two lowest bits of the address are set to zero when an instruction is fetched from memory.

The main reason for imposing the word-boundary restriction is one of efficiency. If an instruction were allowed to straddle two words, two accesses to memory would be required to load a single instruction. As it is, the ARM only ever has to access memory once per instruction fetch. A secondary reason is that by making the two lowest bits of the address implicit, the program address range of the ARM is increased from the 24 bits available in R15 to 26 bits - effectively quadrupling the addressing range.

A 32-bit instruction enables 2^{32} or about 4 billion possible instructions. Obviously the ARM would not be much of a reduced instruction set computer if it used all of these for wildly differing instructions. However, it does use a surprisingly large amount of this theoretical instruction space.

The instruction word may be split into different 'fields'. A field is a set of (perhaps just one) contiguous bits. For example, bits 28 to 31 of R15 could be called the result status field. Each instruction word field controls a particular aspect of the interpretation of the instruction. It is not necessary to know where these fields occur within the word and what they mean, as the assembler does that for you using the textual representation of instruction.

One field which is worth mentioning now is the condition part. Every ARM instruction has a condition code encoded into four bits of the word. Four bits enable up to 16 conditions to be specified, and all of these are used. Most instructions will use the 'unconditional' condition, i.e. they will execute regardless of the state of the flags. Other conditions are 'if zero', 'if carry set', 'if less than' and so on.

Instruction classes

There are five types of instruction. Each class is described in detail in its own section of the next chapter. In summary, they are:

Data operations

This group does most of the work. There are sixteen instructions, and they have very similar formats. Examples of instructions from this group are **ADD** and **CMP**, which add and compare two numbers respectively. As mentioned above, the operands of these instructions are always in registers (or an *immediate* number stored in the instruction itself), never in memory.

Load and save

This is a smaller group of two instructions: load a register and save a register. Variations include whether bytes or words are transferred, and how the memory location to be used is obtained.

Multiple load and save

Whereas the instructions in the previous group only transfer a single register, this group allows between one and 16 registers to be moved between the processor and memory. Only word transfers are performed by this group.

Branching

Although the PC may be altered using the data operations to cause a change in the program counter, the branch instruction provides a convenient way of reaching any part of the 64M byte address space in a single instruction. It causes a *displacement* to be added to the current value of the PC. The displacement is stored in the instruction itself.

SWI

This one-instruction group is very important. The abbreviation stands for 'SoftWare Interrupt'. It provides the way for user's programs to access the facilities provided by the operating system. All ARM-based computers provide a certain amount of pre-written software to perform such tasks as printing characters on to the screen, performing disc I/O etc. By issuing **SWI**

3.1 Condition codes

The property of conditional execution is common to all ARM instructions, so its representation in assembler is described before the syntax of the actual instructions.

As mentioned in chapter two, there are four bits of condition encoded into an instruction word. This allows sixteen possible conditions. If the condition for the current instruction is true, the execution goes ahead. If the condition does not hold, the instruction is ignored and the next one executed.

The result flags are altered mainly by the data manipulation instructions. These instructions only affect the flags if you explicitly tell them to. For example, a **MOV** instruction which copies the contents of one register to another. No flags are affected. However, the **MOVS** (move with **S**et) instruction additionally causes the result flags to be set. The way in which each instruction affects the flags is described below.

To make an instruction conditional, a two-letter suffix is added to the mnemonic. The suffixes, and their meanings, are listed below.

AL Always

An instruction with this suffix is always executed. To save having to type '**AL**' after the majority of instructions which are unconditional, the suffix may be omitted in this case. Thus **ADDAL** and **ADD** mean the same thing: add unconditionally.

NV Never

All ARM conditions also have their inverse, so this is the inverse of always. Any instruction with this condition will be ignored. Such instructions might be used for 'padding' or perhaps to use up a (very) small amount of time in a program.

EQ Equal

This condition is true if the result flag Z (zero) is set. This might arise after a compare instruction where the operands were equal, or in any data instruction which received a zero result into the destination.

NE Not equal

This is clearly the opposite of **EQ**, and is true if the Z flag is cleared. If Z is set, and instruction with the **NE** condition will not be executed.

VS Overflow set

This condition is true if the result flag V (overflow) is set. Add, subtract and compare instructions affect the V flag.

VC Overflow clear

The opposite to **VS**.

MI Minus

Instructions with this condition only execute if the N (negative) flag is set. Such a condition would occur when the last data operation gave a result which was negative. That is, the N flag reflects the state of bit 31 of the result. (All data operations work on 32-bit numbers.)

PL Plus

This is the opposite to the **MI** condition and instructions with the **PL** condition will only execute if the N flag is cleared.

The next four conditions are often used after comparisons of two unsigned numbers. If the numbers being compared are n1 and n2, the conditions are n1>=n2, n1<n2, n1>n2 and n1<=n2, in the order presented.

CS Carry set

This condition is true if the result flag C (carry) is set. The carry flag is affected by arithmetic instructions such as **ADD**, **SUB** and **CMP**. It is also altered by operations involving the shifting or rotation of operands (data manipulation instructions).

When used after a compare instruction, **CS** may be interpreted as 'higher or same', where the operands are treated as unsigned 32-bit numbers. For example, if the left hand operand of **CMP** was 5 and the right hand operand was 2, the carry would be set. You can use **HS** instead of **CS** for this condition.

CC Carry clear

This is the inverse condition to **CS**. After a compare, the **CC** condition may be interpreted as meaning 'lower than', where the operands are again treated as unsigned numbers. An synonym for **CC** is **LO**.

HI Higher

This condition is true if the C flag is set and the Z flag is false. After a compare or subtract, this combination may be interpreted as the left hand operand being greater than the right hand one, where the operands are treated as unsigned.

LS Lower or same

This condition is true if the C flag is cleared or the Z flag is set. After a compare or subtract, this combination may be interpreted as the left hand operand being less than or equal to the right hand one, where the operands are treated as unsigned.

The next four conditions have similar interpretations to the previous four, but are used when signed numbers have been compared. The difference is that they take into account the state of the V (overflow) flag, whereas the unsigned ones don't.

Again, the relationships between the two numbers which would cause the condition to be true are n1>=n2, n1<n2, n1>n2, n1<=n2.

GE Greater than or equal

This is true if N is cleared and V is cleared, or N is set and V is set.

LT Less than

This is the opposite to **GE** and instructions with this condition are executed if N is set and V is cleared, or N is cleared and V is set.

GT Greater than

This is the same as **GE**, with the addition that the Z flag must be cleared too.

LE Less than or equal

This is the same as **LT**, and is also true whenever the Z flag is set.

Note that although the conditions refer to signed and unsigned numbers, the operations on the numbers are identical regardless of the type. The only things that change are the flags used to determine whether instructions are to be obeyed or not.

The flags may be set and cleared explicitly by performing operations directly on R15, where they are stored.

3.2 Group one - data manipulation

This group contains the instructions which do most of the manipulation of data in ARM programs. The other groups are concerned with moving data between the processor and memory, or changing the flow of control.

The group comprises sixteen distinct instructions. All have a very similar format with respect to the operands they take and the 'optional extras'. We shall describe them generically using **ADD**, then give the detailed operation of each type.

Assembler format

ADD has the following format:

```
ADD{cond}{S}  <dest>,  <lhs>,  <rhs>
```

The parts in curly brackets are optional. **Cond** is one of the two-letter condition codes listed above. If it is omitted, the 'always' condition **AL** is assumed. The **S**, if present, causes the instruction to affect the result flags. If there is no **S**, none of the flags will be changed. For example, if an instruction **ADDS** ... yields a result which is negative, then the N flag will be set. However, just **ADD** ... will not alter N (or any other flag) regardless of the result.

After the mnemonic are the three operands. **<dest>** is the destination, and is the register number where the result of the **ADD** is to be stored. Although the assembler is happy with actual numbers here, e.g. 0 for R0, it recognises R0, R1, R2 etc. to stand for the register numbers. In addition, you can define a name for a register and use that instead. For example, in BBC BASIC you could say:-

```
iac = 0
```

where **iac** stands for, say, integer accumulator. Then this can be used in an instruction:-

```
ADD    iac,  iac,  #1
```

The second operand is the left hand side of the operation. In general, the group one instructions act on two values to provide the result. These are referred to as the left and right hand sides, implying that the operation determined by the mnemonic would be written between them in mathematics. For example, the instruction:

```
ADD R0,  R1,  R2
```

has R1 and R2 as its left and right hand sides, and R0 as the result. This is analogous to an assignment such as **R0=R1+R2** in BASIC, so the operands are sometimes said to be in 'assignment order'.

The **<lhs>** operand is always a register number, like the destination. The **<rhs>** may either be a register, or an immediate operand, or a shifted or rotated register. It is the versatile form that the right hand side may take which gives much of the power to these instructions.

If the `<rhs>` is a simple register number, we obtain instructions such as the first **ADD** example above. In this case, the contents of R1 and R2 are added (as signed, 32-bit numbers) and the result stored in R0. As there is no condition after the instruction, the **ADD** instruction will always be executed. Also, because there was no **S**, the result flags would not be affected.

The three examples below all perform the same **ADD** operation (if the condition is true):

```
ADDNE   R0,  R0,  R2
ADDS    R0,  R0,  R2
ADDNES  R0,  R0,  R2
```

They all add R2 to R0. The first has a **NE** condition, so the instruction will only be executed if the Z flag is cleared. If Z is set when the instruction is encountered, it is ignored. The second one is unconditional, but has the **S** option. Thus the N, Z, V and C flags will be altered to reflect the result. The last example has the condition and the **S**, so if Z is cleared, the **ADD** will occur and the flags set accordingly. If Z is set, the **ADD** will be skipped and the flags remain unaltered.

Immediate operands

Immediate operands are written as a **#** followed by a number. For example, to increment R0, we would use:

```
ADD     R0,  R0,  #1
```

Now, as we know, an ARM instruction has 32 bits in which to encode the instruction type, condition, operands etc. In group one instructions there are twelve bits available to encode immediate operands. Twelve bits of binary can represent numbers in the range 0..4095, or -2048..+2047 if we treat them as signed.

The designers of the ARM decided not to use the 12 bits available to them for immediate operands in the obvious way just mentioned. Remember that some of the status bits are stored in bits 26..31 of R15. If we wanted to store an immediate value there using a group one instruction, there's no way we could using the straightforward twelve-bit number approach.

To get around this and related problems, the immediate operand is split into two fields, called the position (the top four bits) and the value (stored in the lower eight bits). The value is an eight bit number representing 256 possible combinations. The position is a four bit field which determines where in the

32-bit word the value lies. Below is a diagram showing how the sixteen values of the position determine where the value goes. The bits of the value part are shown as 0, 1, 2 etc.

The way of describing this succinctly is to say that the value is rotated by 2*position bits to the right within the 32-bit word. As you can see from the diagram, when position=&03, all of the status bits in R15 can be reached.

```
|Bit 31                        Bit 0|    Position
|                                   |
........................76543210         &00
10........................765432         &01
3210........................7654         &02
543210........................76         &03
76543210........................         &04
..76543210......................         &05
....76543210....................         &06
......76543210..................         &07
........76543210................         &08
..........76543210..............         &09
............76543210............         &0A
..............76543210..........         &0B
................76543210........         &0C
..................76543210......         &0D
....................76543210....         &0E
......................76543210..         &0F
```

The sixteen immediate shift positions

When using immediate operands, you don't have to specify the number in terms of position and value. You just give the number you want, and the assembler tries to generate the appropriate twelve-bit field. If you specify a value which can't be generated, such as &101 (which would require a nine-bit value), an error is generated. The **ADD** instruction below adds 65536 (&1000) to R0:

```
ADD     R0, R0, #&1000
```

To get this number, the assembler might use a position value of 8 and value of 1, though other combinations could also be used.

Shifted operands

If the **<rhs>** operand is a register, it may be manipulated in various ways before it is used in the instruction. The contents of the register aren't altered, just the value given to the ALU, as applied to this operation (unless the same register is also used as the result, of course).

The particular operations that may be performed on the **<rhs>** are various types of shifting and rotation. The number of bits by which the register is shifted or rotated may be given as an immediate number, or specified in yet another register.

Shifts and rotates are specified as left or right, logical or arithmetic. A left shift is one where the bits, as written on the page, are moved by one or more bits to the left, i.e. towards the more significant end. Zero-valued bits are shifted in at the right and the bits at the left are lost, except for the final bit to be shifted out, which is stored in the carry flag.

Left shifts by n bits effectively multiply the number by 2^n, assuming that no significant bits are 'lost' at the top end.

A right shift is in the opposite direction, the bits moving from the more significant end to the lower end, or from left to right on the page. Again the bits shifted out are lost, except for the last one which is put into the carry. If the right shift is logical then zeros are shifted into the left end. In arithmetic shifts, a copy of bit 31 (i.e. the sign bit) is shifted in.

Right arithmetic shifts by n bits effectively divide the number by 2^n, rounding towards minus infinity (like the BASIC **INT** function).

A rotate is like a shift except that the bits shifted in to the left (right) end are those which are coming out of the right (left) end.

Here are the types of shifts and rotates which may be used:

LSL #n   Logical shift left immediate

n is the number of bit positions by which the value is shifted. It has the value 0..31. An **LSL** by one bit may be pictured as below:

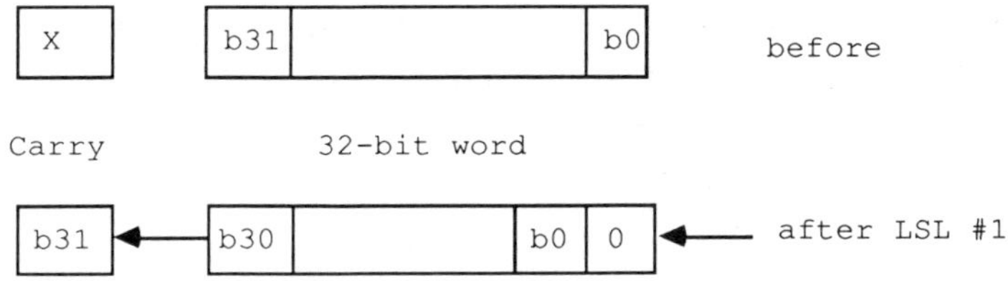

After n shifts, n zero bits have been shifted in on the right and the carry is set to bit 32-n of the original word.

Note that if there is no shift specified after the **<rhs>** register value, **LSL #0** is used, which has no effect at all.

ASL #n Arithmetic shift left immediate

This is a synonym for **LSL #n** and has an identical effect.

LSR #n Logical shift right immediate

n is the number of bit positions by which the value is shifted. It has the value 1..32. An **LSR** by one bit is shown below:

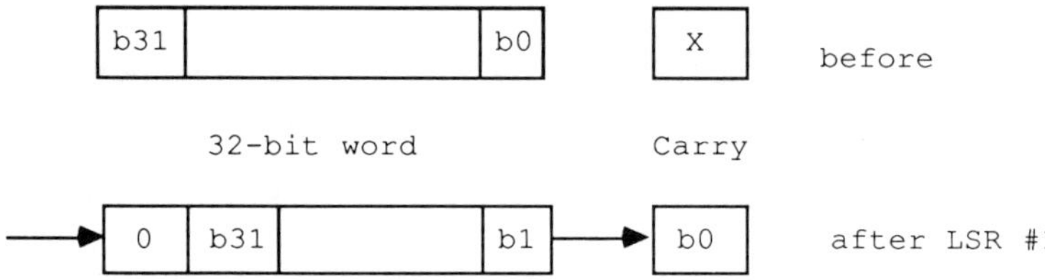

After n of these, n zero bits have been shifted in on the left, and the carry flag is set to bit n-1 of the original word.

ASR #n Arithmetic shift right immediate

n is the number of bit positions by which the value is shifted. It has the value 1..32. An **ASR** by one bit is shown below:

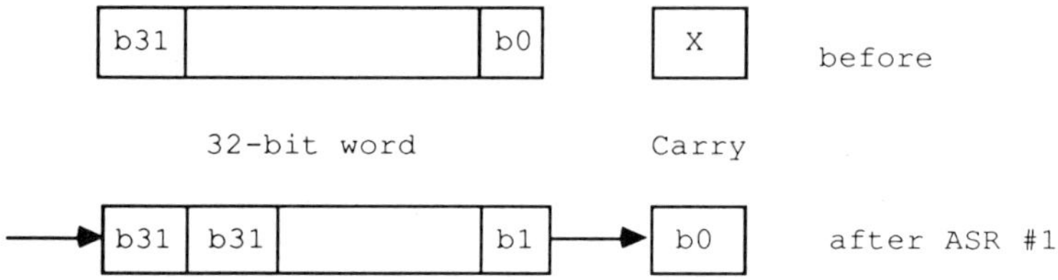

If ' sign' is the original value of bit 31 then after n shifts, n 'sign' bits have been shifted in on the left, and the carry flag is set to bit n-1 of the original word.

ROR #n Rotate right immediate

n is the number of bit positions to rotate in the range 1..31. A rotate right by one bit is shown below:

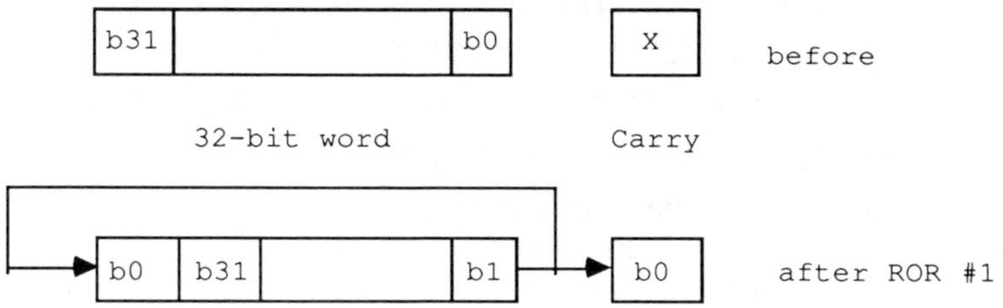

After n of these rotates, the old bit n is in the bit 0 position; the old bit (n-1) is in bit 31 and in the carry flag.

Note that a rotate left by n positions is the same as a rotate right by (32-n). Also note that there is no rotate right by 32 bits. The instruction code which would do this has been reserved for rotate right with extend (see below).

RRX Rotate right one bit with extend

This special case of rotate right has a slightly different effect from the usual rotates. There is no count; it always rotates by one bit only. The pictorial representation of **RRX** is:

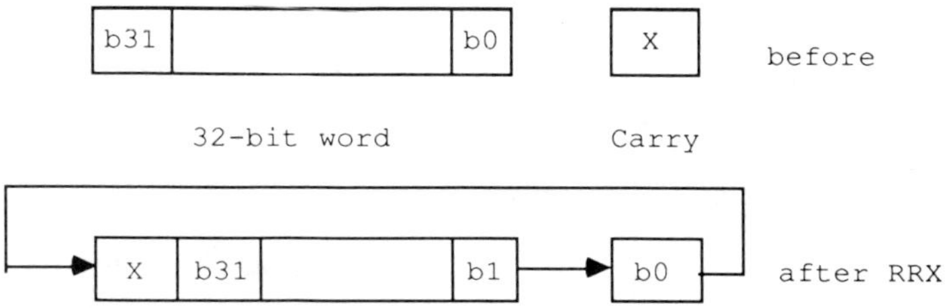

The old bit 0 is shifted into the carry. The old content of the carry is shifted into bit 31.

Note that there is no equivalent **RLX** rotate. However, the same effect may be obtained using the instruction:

```
ADCS    R0,R0,R0
```

After this, the carry will contain the old bit 31 of R0, and bit 0 of R0 will contain the old carry flag.

LSL rn Logical shift left by a register.
ASL rn Arithmetic shift left by a register.
LSR rn Logical shift right by a register.
ASR rn Arithmetic shift right by a register.
ROR rn Rotate right by a register

This group acts like the immediate shift group, but takes the count from the contents of a specified register instead of an immediate value. Only the least significant byte of the register is used, so the shift count is in the range 0..255. Of course, only counts in the range 0..32 are useful anyway.

We now have the complete syntax of group one instructions:

```
ADD{cond}{S}  <dest>,<lhs>,<rhs>
```

where **<dest>** and **<lhs>** are registers, and **<rhs>** is:

```
#<value>   or
<reg>  {,<shift>}
```

where **<value>** is a shifted immediate number as explained above, **<reg>** is a register and **<shift>** is:

```
<shift type> #<shift count> or
<shift type> <reg> or
RRX
```

where **<shift type>** is **LSL**, **ASL**, **LSR**, **ASR**, **ROR** and **<shift count>** is in the range 0..32, depending on the shift type.

Here is an example of the **ADD** instruction using shifted operands:

```
ADD    R0, R0, R0, LSL #1    ;R0 = R0+2*R0 = 3*R0
```

Instruction descriptions

The foregoing applies to all group one instructions. We now list and explain the individual operations in the group. They may be divided into two sub-groups: logical and arithmetic. These differ in the way in which the result flags are affected (assuming the **S** is present in the mnemonic). Arithmetic instructions alter N, Z, V and C according to the result of the addition, subtraction etc.

Logical instructions affect N and Z according to the result of the operation, and C according to any shifts or rotates that occurred in the **<rhs>**. For example, the instruction:

```
ANDS    R0,R1,R2, LSR #1
```

will set C from bit 0 of R2. Immediate operands will generally leave the carry unaffected if the position value is 0 (i.e. an operand in the range 0..255). For other immediate values, the state of C is hard to predict after the instruction, and it is probably best not to assume anything about the state of the carry after a logical operation which uses the **S** option and has an immediate operand.

To summarise the state of the result flags after any logical operation, if the **S** option was not given, then there is no change to the flags. Otherwise:

If result is negative (bit 31=1), N is set, otherwise it is cleared.
If result is zero, Z is set, otherwise it is cleared.
If **<rhs>** involved a shift or rotate, C is set from this, otherwise it is unaffected by the operation.

V is unaffected

AND Logical AND

The **AND** instruction produces the bit-wise AND of its operands. The AND of two bits is 1 only if both of the bits are 1, as summarised below:

<lhs>	<rhs>	<lhs> AND <rhs>
0	0	0
0	1	0
1	0	0
1	1	1

In the ARM **AND** instruction, this operation is applied to all 32 bits in the operands. That is, bit 0 of the **<lhs>** is **AND**ed with bit 0 of the **<rhs>** and stored in bit 0 of the **<dest>**, and so on.

Examples:

```
ANDS    R0, R0, R5    ;Mask wanted bits using R5
AND     R0, R0, #&DF  ;Convert character to upper case
```

BIC Clear specified bits

The **BIC** instruction produces the bit-wise **AND** of **<lhs>** and **NOT <rhs>**. This has the effect of clearing the **<lhs>** bit if the **<rhs>** bit is set, and leaving the **<lhs>** bit unaltered otherwise.

```
<lhs>  <rhs>    NOT <rhs>   <lhs> AND NOT <rhs>
  0      0         1              0
  0      1         0              0
  1      0         1              1
  1      1         0              0
```

In the ARM **BIC** instruction, this operation is applied to all bits in the operands. That is, bit 0 of the **<lhs>** is **AND**ed with **NOT** bit 0 of the **<rhs>** and stored in bit 0 of the **<dest>**, and so on.

Examples:

```
BICS    R0,R0,R5   ;Zero unwanted bits using R5
BIC     R0,R0,#&20 ;Convert to caps by clearing bit 5
```

TST Test bits

The **TST** instruction performs the AND operation on its **<lhs>** and **<rhs>** operands. The result is not stored anywhere, but the result flags are set according to the result. As there are only two operands, the format of **TST** is:

```
TST     <lhs>,<rhs>
```

Also, as the only purpose of executing a **TST** is to set the flags according to the result, the assembler assumes the **S** is present whether you specify it or not, i.e. **TST** always affects the flags.

See the section 'Using R15 in group one instructions' below.

Examples:

```
TST     R0,R5      ;Test bits using r5, setting flags
TST     R0,#&20    ;Test case of character in R0
```

ORR Logical OR

The **ORR** instruction produces the bit-wise OR of its operands. The OR of two bits is 1 if either or both of the bits is 1, as summarised below:

```
<lhs> <rhs>  <lhs> OR <rhs>
  0     0         0
  0     1         1
  1     0         1
  1     1         1
```

In the ARM **ORR** instruction, this operation is applied to all bits in the operands. That is, bit 0 of the **<lhs>** is ORed with bit 0 of the **<rhs>** and stored in bit 0 of the **<dest>**, and so on. This instruction is often used to set specific bits in a register without affecting the others. It can be regarded as a complementary operation to **BIC**.

Examples:

```
ORRS    R0,R0,R5    ;Set desired bits using R5
ORR     R0,R0,&80000000 ;Set top bit of R0
```

EOR Logical exclusive-OR

The **EOR** instruction produces the bit-wise exclusive-OR of its operands. The EOR of two bits is 1 only if they are different, as summarised below:

```
<lhs> <rhs> <lhs> EOR <rhs>
  0     0         0
  0     1         1
  1     0         1
  1     1         0
```

In the ARM **EOR** instruction, this operation is applied to all bits in the operands. That is, bit 0 of the **<lhs>** is EORed with bit 0 of the **<rhs>** and stored in bit 0 of the **<dest>**, and so on. The **EOR** instruction is often used to invert the state of certain bits of a register without affecting the rest.

Examples:

```
EORS    R0,R0,R5    ;Invert bits using R5, setting flags
EOR     R0,R0,#1    ;'Toggle' state of bit 0
```

TEQ Test equivalence

The **TEQ** instruction performs the EOR operation on its **<lhs>** and **<rhs>** operands. The result is not stored anywhere, but the result flags are set according to the result. As there are only two operands, the format of **TEQ** is:

```
TEQ     <lhs>,<rhs>
```

Also, as the only purpose of executing a **TEQ** is to set the flags according to the result, the assembler assumes the **S** is present whether you specify or not, i.e. **TEQ** always affects the flags.

One use of **TEQ** is to test if two operands are equal without affecting the state of the C flag, as the **CMP** instruction does (see below). After such an operation, Z=1 if the operands are equal, or 0 if not. The second example below illustrates this.

See the section 'Using R15 in group one instructions' below.

Examples:

```
TEQ R0,R5       ;Test bits using R5, setting flags
TEQ R0,#0       ;See if R0 = 0.
```

MOV Move value

The **MOV** instruction transfers its **<rhs>** operand to the register specified by **<dest>**. There is no **<lhs>** specified in the instruction, so the assembler format is:

```
MOV     <dest>,<rhs>
```

Examples:

```
MOV     R0, R0,LSL #2 ;Multiply R0 by four.
MOVS    R0, R1        ;Put R1 in R0, setting flags
MOV     R1, #&80      ;Set R1 to 128
```

MVN Move value

The **MOV** instruction transfers the logical **NOT** of its **<rhs>** operand to the register specified by **<dest>**. Inverting the **<rhs>** before transfer enables negative immediate operands to be loaded. There is no **<lhs>** specified in the instruction, so the assembler format is:

```
MVN     <dest>,<rhs>
```

In general, -n = NOT (n-1). This means that to load a negative number, you subtract one from its positive value and use that in the **MVN**. For example, to load the number -128 you would do a **MVN** of 127.

Examples:

```
MVNS    R0, R0     ;Invert all bits of R0, setting flags
MVN     R0, #0     ;Set R0 to &FFFFFFFF, i.e. -1
```

Descriptions of the arithmetic instructions follow. Here is a summary of how the result flags are affected by these instructions. If the **S** option is not specified, no change takes place. Otherwise:

If result is negative (bit 31=1), N is set, otherwise it is cleared.
If result is zero, Z is set, otherwise it is cleared.
If the operation generated a carry, C is set, otherwise it is cleared.
If the operation generated an overflow, V is set, otherwise it is cleared.

Note that if C=1 after an **ADDS**, the implication is that a carry was generated, i.e. the addition overflowed into bit 32. This does not mean that the result is wrong. For example, adding -1 to 10 will produce the following:–

```
    00000000000000000000000000001010
+   11111111111111111111111111111111
    ________________________________
    00000000000000000000000000001001
  1 ________________________________
```

A carry is generated, but the result we obtain is the desired one, i.e. 9. The overflow flag (see below) is used for detecting errors in the arithmetic. In this case, V=0 after the operation, implying no overflow.

The state of the carry after a **SUBS** is the opposite to that after an **ADDS**. If C=1, no borrow was generated during the subtract. If C=0, a borrow was required. Note that by this definition, borrow = **NOT** carry, so the summary of the flags' states above is correct.

The precise definition of the overflow state is the exclusive-**OR** of the carries from bits 30 and 31 during the add or subtract operation. What this means in real terms is that if the V flag is set, the result is too large to fit in a single 32-bit word. In this case, the sign of the result will be wrong, which is why the signed condition codes take the state of the V flag into account.

ADD Addition

This instruction adds the **<lhs>** operand to the **<rhs>** operand, storing the result in **<dest>**. The addition is a thirty-two bit signed operation, though if the operands are treated as unsigned numbers, then the result can be too.

Examples:

```
    ADD     R0,R0,#1            ;Increment R0
    ADD     R0,R0,R0,LSL#2      ;Multiple R0 by 5
    ADDS    R2,R2,R7            ;Add result; check for overflow
```

ADC Addition with carry

The add with carry operation is very similar to **ADD**, with the difference that the carry flag is added too. Whereas the function of **ADD** can be written:

```
    <dest> = <lhs> + <rhs>
```

we must add an extra part for **ADC**:

```
    <dest> = <lhs> + <rhs> + <carry>
```

where **<carry>** is 0 if C is cleared and 1 if it is set. The purpose of **ADC** is to allow multi-word addition to take place, as the example illustrates.

Example:

```
;Add the 64-bit number in R2,R3 to that in R0,R1
    ADDS    R0,R0,R2    ;Add the lower words, getting carry
    ADC     R1,R1,R3    ;Add upper words, using carry
```

SUB Subtract

This instruction subtracts the **<rhs>** operand from the **<lhs>** operand, storing the result in **<dest>**. The subtraction is a thirty-two bit signed operation.

Examples:

```
    SUB     R0,R0,#1         ;Decrement R0
    SUB     R0,R0,R0,ASR#2   ;Multiply R0 by 3/4 (R0=R0-R0/4)
```

SBC Subtract with carry

This has the same relationship to **SUB** as **ADC** has to **ADD**. The operation may be written:

```
    <dest> = <lhs> - <rhs> - NOT <carry>
```

Notice that the carry is inverted because the C flag is cleared by a subtract that needed a borrow and set by one that didn't. As long as multi-word subtracts are performed using **SUBS** for the lowest word and **SBCS** for subsequent ones, the way in which the carry is set shouldn't concern the programmer.

Example:

```
;Subtract the 64-bit number in R2,R3 from that in R0,R1
    SUBS    R0,R0,R2    ;Sub the lower words, getting borrow
    SBC     R1,R1,R3    ;Sub upper words, using borrow
```

RSB Reverse subtract

This instruction performs a subtract without carry, but reverses the order in which its operands are subtracted. The instruction:

```
    RSB     <dest>,<lhs>,<rhs>
```

performs the operation:

```
    <dest> = <rhs> - <lhs>
```

The instruction is provided so that the full power of the **<rhs>** operand (register, immediate, shifted register) may be used on either side of a subtraction. For example, in order to obtain the result 1-R1 in the register R0, you would have to use:

```
    MVN     R0,R1       ;get NOT (R1) = -R1-1
    ADD     R0,R0,#2    ;get -R1-1+2 = 1-R1
```

However, using **RSB** this could be written:

```
    RSB     R0, R1, #1 ;R0 = 1 - R0
```

In more complex examples, extra registers might be needed to hold temporary results if subtraction could only operate in one direction.

Example:

```
;Multiply R0 by 7
    RSB     R0, R0, R0, ASL #3    ;Get 8*R0-R0 = 7*R0
```

RSC Reverse subtract with carry

This is the 'with carry' version of **RSB**. Its operation is:

```
    <dest> = <rhs> - <lhs> - NOT <carry>
```

It is used to perform multiple-word reversed subtracts.

Example

```
    ;Obtain &100000000-R0,R1 in R0,R1
    RSBS    R0,R0,#0   ;Sub the lower words, getting borrow
    RSC     R1, R1,#1  ;Sub the upper words
```

CMP Compare

The **CMP** instruction is used to compare two numbers. It does this by subtracting one from the other, and setting the status flags according to the result. Like **TEQ** and **TST**, **CMP** doesn't actually store the result anywhere. Its format is:

```
    CMP     <lhs>, <rhs>
```

Also like **TST** and **TEQ** it doesn't require the **S** option to be set, as **CMP** without setting the flags wouldn't do anything at all.

After a **CMP**, the various conditions can be used to execute instructions according to the relationship between the integers. Note that the two operands being compared may be regarded as either signed (two's complement) or unsigned quantities, depending on which of the conditions is used.

See the section 'Using R15 in group one instructions' below.

Examples:

```
    CMP     R0,#&100        ;Check R0 takes a single byte

    CMP     R0,R1           ;Get greater of R1, R0 in R0
    MOVLT   R0,R1
```

CMN Compare negative

The **CMN** instruction compares two numbers, but negates the right hand side before performing the comparison. The 'subtraction' performed is therefore **<lhs>--<rhs>**, or simply **<lhs>+<rhs>**. The main use of **CMN** is in comparing a register with a small negative immediate number, which would not otherwise be possible without loading the number into a register (using **MVN**). For example, a comparison with -1 would require

```
MVN     R1,#0       ;Get -1 in R1
CMP     R0,R1       ;Do the comparison
```

which uses two instructions and an auxiliary register, compared to this:

```
CMN     R0,#1       ;Compare R0 with -1
```

Note that whereas **MVN** is 'move *NOT*', **CMN** is 'compare *negative*', so there is a slight difference in the way **<rhs>** is altered before being used in the operation.

See the section 'Using R15 in group one instructions' below.

Example

```
CMN     R0,#256         ;Make sure R0 >= -256
MVNLT   R0,#255
```

Using R15 in group one instructions

As we know, R15 is a general-purpose register, and as such may be cited in any situation where a register is required as an operand. However, it is also used for storing both the program counter and the status register. Because of this, there are some special rules which have to be obeyed when you use R15. These are described in this section.

The first rule concerns how much of R15 is 'visible' when it is used as one of the source operands, i.e. in an **<rhs>** or **<lhs >** position. Simply stated, it is:

if **<lhs>** is R15 then only bits 2..25 (the PC) are visible
if **<rhs>** is R15 then all bits 0..31 are visible

So, in the instruction:

```
ADD     R0,R15,#128
```

the result of adding 128 to the PC is stored in R0. The eight status bits of R15 are seen as zeros by the ALU, and so they don't figure in the addition. Remember also that the value of the PC that is presented to the ALU during the addition is eight greater than the address of the **ADD** itself, because of pipelining (this is described in more detail below).

In the instruction

```
MOV     R0,R15,ROR  #26
```

all 32 bits of R15 are used, as this time the register is being used in an **<rhs>** position. The effect of this instruction is to obtain the eight status bits in the least significant byte of R0.

The second rule concerns using R15 as the destination operand. In the instruction descriptions above we stated that (if **S** is present) the status bits N, Z, C and C are determined by the outcome of the instruction. For example, a result of zero would cause the Z bit to be set.

In the cases when R15 itself is the destination register, this behaviour changes. If **S** is not given in the instruction, only the PC bits of R15 are affected, as usual. So the instruction

```
ADD     R15,R15,R0
```

adds some displacement which is stored in R0 to the program counter, leaving the status unaffected.

If **S** is present in the instruction, and the instruction isn't one of **TST**, **TEQ**, **CMP**, or **CMN** (which are explained below), the status bits which are allowed to be altered in the current processor mode are overwritten directly by the result. (As opposed to the status of the result.) An example should make this clear. To explicitly set the carry flag (bit 29 of R15) we might use:

```
ORRS    R15,R15,#&20000000
```

Now, as the second R15 is in a **<lhs>** position, the status bits are presented as zeros to the ALU (because of the first rule described above). Thus the value written into the status register is (in binary) 001000...00. In fact, in user modes, only the top four bits may be affected (i.e. the interrupt masks and processor mode bits can't be altered in user mode).

The example above has the (usually) unfortunate side effect of skipping the two instructions which follow the **ORR**. This is, as usual, due to pipelining. The R15 value which is transferred into the ALU holds the address of the third instruction after the current one, thus the intervening two are never executed. (They are pre-fetched into pipeline, but whenever the PC is altered, the ARM has to disregard the current pre-fetched instructions.)

To overcome this there is a special way of writing to the status bits, and only the status bits, of R15. It involves using the four instructions which don't usually have a destination register: **TST**, **TEQ**,, **CMP**, and **CMN**. As we know, these usually affect the flags from the result of the operation because they have an implicit **S** option built-in. Also, usually the assembler makes the **<dest>** part of the instruction code R0 (it still has this field in the instruction, even if it isn't given in the assembly language).

Now, if the **<dest>** field of one of these instructions is made R15 instead, a useful thing happens. The status bits are updated from the result of the operation (the **AND**, **EOR**, **SUB** or**ADD** as appropriate), but the PC part remains unaltered.

The problem is how to make the assembler use R15 in the **<dest>** field instead of R0. This is done by adding a **P** to the instruction. To give a concrete example, we will show how the carry flag can be set *without* skipping over the next two instructions:

```
TEQP    R15,#&20000000
```

This works as follows. The R15 is a **<lhs>** so the status bits appear as zeros to the ALU. Thus **EOR**ing the mask for the carry flag with this results in that bit being set when the result is transferred to R15. The rest of the status register (or at least the bits which are alterable) will be cleared.

Setting and clearing only selected status bits while leaving the rest alone takes a bit more effort. First the current value of the bits must be obtained. Then the appropriate masking is performed and the result stored in R15. For example, to clear the overflow flag (bit 28) while preserving the rest, something like this is needed:

```
MOV     tmp,R15         ;Get the status
BIC     tmp,tmp,#1<<28;Clear bit 28
TEQP    R15,tmp         ;Store the new status
```

Finally, we have to say something about performing arithmetic on R15 in order to alter the execution path of the program. As we will see later in this chapter, there is a special **B** (for Branch) instruction, which causes the PC to take on a new value, This causes a jump to another part of the program, similar to the BASIC **GOTO** statement. However, by changing the value of R15 using group one instructions such as **ADD**, we can achieve more versatile control, for example emulating the BASIC **ON..GOTO** statement.

The important thing to bear in mind when dealing with the PC has already been mentioned once or twice: the effect of pipelining. The value obtained when R15 is used as an operand is 8 bytes, or 2 words, greater than the address of the current instruction. Thus if the instruction

```
MOV     R0,R15
```

was located at address &8000, then the value loaded into R15 would be &8008. Chapters Five and Six contain several examples of the use of R15 where pipelining is taken into account.

Group One A

There is a small class of instructions which is similar in form to the group one instructions, but doesn't belong in that group. These are the multiply instructions, whose form bears a similarity to the simplest form of group one instructions.

Two distinct operations make up this group, multiply and multiply with accumulate. The formats are:

```
MUL{cond}{S}   <dest,<lhs>,<rhs>
MLA{cond}{S}   <dest>,<lhs>,<rhs>,<add>
```

All operands are simple registers; there are no immediate operands or shifted registers. **MUL** multiplies **<lhs>** by **<rhs>** and stores the result in **<dest>**. MLA does the same, but adds register **<add>** before storing the result.

You must obey certain restrictions on the operands when using these instructions. The registers used for **<rhs>** and **<dest>** must be different. Additionally, you should not use R15 as a destination, as this would produce a meaningless result. In fact, R15 is protected from modification by the multiply instructions. There are no other restrictions.

If the **S** option is specified, the flags are affected as follows. The N and Z flags are set to reflect the status of the result register, the same as the rest of the group one instructions. The overflow flag is unaltered, and the carry flag is undefined.

You can regard the operands of the multiply instructions as unsigned or as two's complement signed numbers. In both cases, the correct results will be obtained.

Example:

```
MUL     R0,R1,R2
```

Summary of group one

The group one instructions have the following form:

```
<op1>{cond}{S}{P}       <dest>,<lhs>,<rhs>
<op2>{cond}{S}{P}       <dest>,<rhs>
<op3>{cond}{S}{P}       <lhs>,<rhs>
```

where **<op1>** is one of **ADD**, **ADC**, **AND**, **BIC**, **EOR**, **ORR**, **RSB**, **RSC**, **SBC**, **SUB**, **<op2>** is one of **MOV**, **MVN**, and **<op3>** is one of **TEQ**, **TST**,**CMN**, **CMP**.

The following **<op3>**s have no **<dest>** field: **CMN**, **CMP**, **TEQ**, **TST**. They allow the use of the **{P}** option to set the **<dest>** field in the machine code to R15 instead of the default R0.

The following **<op2>**s have no **<lhs>** field: **MOV**, **MVN**.

<dest> and **<lhs>** are registers.

<rhs> is **#<expression>** where **<expression>** is a 12-bit shifted immediate operand
or:
<register>
or:
<register>, <shift type> <count>

where **<shift type>** is **LSL**, **ASL**, **ASR**, **LSR**, **ROR** and where **<count>** is **#<expression>** or **<register>** where **<expression>** is five-bit unsigned value,
or:
<register>, RRX

3.3 Group two - load and store

We turn now to the first set of instructions concerned with getting data in and out of the processor. There are only two basic instructions in this category. **LDR** loads a register from a specified location and **STR** saves a register.

As with group one, there are several options which make the instructions very versatile. As the main difference between **LDR** and **STR** is the direction in which the data is transferred (i.e. to or from the processor), we will explain only one of the instructions in detail - **STR**. Notes about **LDR** follow this description.

STR Store a word or byte

Addressing modes

When storing data into memory, you have to be able to specify the desired location. There are two main ways of giving the address, called addressing modes. These are known as pre-indexed and post-indexed addressing.

Pre-indexed addressing

Pre-indexed addressing is specified as below:

```
STR{cond}  <srce>,[<base>{,<offset>}]
```

<srce> is the register from which the data is to be transferred to memory. **<base>** is a register containing the base address of memory location required. **<offset>** is an optional number which is added to the address before the data is stored. So the address actually used to store the **<srce>** data is **<base>+<offset>**

Offset formats

The **<offset>** is specified in one of two ways. It may be an immediate number in the range 0 to 4095, or a (possibly) shifted register. For example:

```
STR     R0,[R1,#20]
```

will store R0 at byte address R1+20. The offset may be specified as negative, in which case it is subtracted from the base address. An example is:

```
STR     R0,[R1,#-200]
```

which stores R0 at R1-200.

(Note for alert readers. The immediate offset is stored as a 12-bit magnitude plus one bit 'direction', not as a 13-bit two's complement number. Therefore the offset range really is -4095 to +4095, not -4096 to +4095, as you might expect.)

If the offset is specified as a register, it has the same syntax as the **<rhs>** of group one instructions. That is, it could be a simple register contents, or the contents of a register shifted or rotated by an immediate number.

Note: the offset register can only have an immediate shift applied to it. In this respect, the offset differs from the **<rhs>** of group one instructions. The latter can also have a shift which is stored in a register.

This example stores R0 in the address given by R1+R2*4:

```
STR     R0,[R1,R2,LSL#2]
```

Again, the offset may be negative as this example illustrates:

```
STR     R0,[R1,-R2,LSL#3]
```

Write-back

Quite frequently, once the address has been calculated, it is convenient to update the base register from it. This enables it to be used in the next instruction. This is useful when stepping through memory at a fixed offset. By adding a **!** to the end of the instruction, you can force the base register to be updated from the **<base>+<offset>** calculation. An example is:

```
STR     R0,[R1,#-16]!
```

This will store R0 at address R1-16, and then perform an automatic:

```
SUB     R1,R1,#16
```

which, because of the way in which the ARM works, does not require any extra time.

Byte and word operations

All of the examples of **STR** we have seen so far have assumed that the final address is on a word boundary, i.e. is a multiple of 4. This is a constraint that you must obey when using the **STR** instruction. However, it is possible to store single bytes which may be located at any address. The byte form of **STR** is obtained by adding **B** at the end. For example:

```
STRB    R0,[R1,#1]!
```

will store the least significant byte of R0 at address R1+1 and store this address in R1 (as **!** is used).

Post-indexed addressing

The second addressing mode that **STR** and **LDR** use is called post-indexed addressing. In this mode, the **<offset>** isn't added to the **<base>** until after the instruction has executed. The general format of a post-indexed **STR** is:

```
STR{cond}  <srce>,[<base>],<offset>
```

The **<base>** and **<offset>** operands have the same format as pre-indexed addressing. Note though that the **<offset>** is always present, and write-back always occurs (so no **!** is needed). Thus the instruction:

```
STRB    R0,[R1],R2
```

will save the least significant byte of R0 at address R1. Then R1 is set to R1+R2. The **<offset>** is used only to update the **<base>** register at the end of the instruction. An example with an immediate **<offset>** is:

```
STR     R2,[R4],#-16
```

which stores R2 at the address held in R4, then decrements R4 by 4 words.

LDR Load a word or byte

The **LDR** instruction is similar in most respects to **STR**. The main difference is, of course, that the register operand is loaded from the given address, instead of saved to it.

The addressing modes are identical, and the **B** option to load a single byte (padded with zeros) into the least significant byte of the register is provided.

When an attempt is made to **LDR** a word from a non-word boundary, special corrective action is taken. If the load address is **addr**, then the word at **addr AND &3FFFFFFC** is loaded. That is, the two least significant bits of the address are set to zero, and the contents of that word address are accessed. Then, the register is rotated right by **(addr MOD 4)*8** bits. To see why this is done, consider the following example. Suppose the contents of address &1000 is &76543210. The table below shows the contents of R0 after a word load from various addresses:

Address	R0
&1000	&76543210
&1001	&10765432
&1002	&32107654
&1003	&54321076

After the rotation, at least the least significant byte of R0 contains the correct value. When **addr** is &1000, it is a word-boundary load and the complete word is as expected. When **addr** is &1001, the first three bytes are as expected, but the last byte is the contents of &1000, rather than the desired &1004. This (at first sight) odd behaviour facilitates writing code to perform word loads on arbitrary byte boundaries. It also makes the implementation of extra hardware to perform correct non-word-aligned loads easier.

Note that **LDR** and **STR** will never affect the status bits, even if **<dest>** or **<base>** is R15. Also, if R15 is used as the base register, pipelining means that the value used will be eight bytes higher than the address of the instruction. This is taken into account automatically when PC-relative addressing is used.

PC relative addressing

The assembler will accept a special form of pre-indexed address in the **LDR** instruction, which is simply:

```
LDR     <dest>,<expression>
```

where **<expression>** yields an address. In this case, the instruction generated will use R15 (i.e. the program counter) as the base register, and calculate the immediate offset automatically. If the address given is not in the correct range (-4095 to +4095) from the instruction, an error is given.

An example of this form of instruction is:

```
LDR     R0,default
```

(We assume that **default** is a label in the program. Labels are described more fully in the next chapter, but for now suffice is to say that they are set to the address of the point in the program where they are defined.)

As the assembler knows the value of the PC when the program is executed, it can calculate the immediate offset required to access the location **default**. This must be within the range -4095 to +4095 of course. This form of addressing is used frequently to access constants embedded in the program.

Summary of LDR and STR

Below is a summary of the syntax for the register load and save instructions.

```
<op>{cond}{B}  <dest>,[<base>{,#<imm>}]{!}

<op>{cond}{B}  <dest>,[<base>,{+|-}<off>{,<shift>}]{!}

<op>{cond}{B}  <dest>,<expression>

<op>{cond}{B}  <dest>,[<base>],#<imm>

<op>{cond}{B}  <dest>,[<base>],{+|-}<off>{,<shift>}
```

Although we haven't used any explicit examples, it is implicit given the regularity of the ARM instruction set that any **LDR** or **STR** instruction may be made conditional by adding the two letter code. Any **B** option follows this.

<op> means **LDR** or **STR**. **<imm>** means an immediate value between -4095 and +4095. **{+|-}** means an optional + or - sign may be present. **<off>** is the offset register number. **<base>** is a base register, and **<shift>** refers to the standard immediate (but *not* register shift) described in the section above on group one instructions.

Note that the case of:

```
STR     R0,label
```

is covered. Although the assembler will accept this and generate the appropriate PC-relative instruction, its use implies that the program is writing over or near its code. Generally this is not advisable because (a) it may lead inadvertently to over-writing the program with dire consequences, and (b) if the program is to be placed in ROM, it will cease to function, as ROMs are generally read-only devices, on the whole.

3.4 Group three - multiple load and store

The previous instruction group was eminently suitable for transferring single data items in and out of the ARM processor. However, circumstances often arise where several registers need to be saved (or loaded) at once. For example, a program might need to save the contents of R1 to R12 while these registers are used for some calculation, then load them back when the result has been obtained. The sequence:

```
STR R1, [R0],#4
STR R2, [R0],#4
STR R3, [R0],#4
STR R4, [R0],#4
STR R5, [R0],#4
STR R6, [R0],#4
STR R7, [R0],#4
STR R8, [R0],#4
STR R9, [R0],#4
STR R10, [R0],#4
STR R11, [R0],#4
STR R12, [R0],#4
```

to save them is inefficient in terms of both space and time. The **LDM** (load multiple) and **STM** (store multiple) instructions are designed to perform tasks such as the one above in an efficient manner.

As with **LDR** and **STR** we will describe one variant in detail, followed by notes on the differences in the other. First though, a word about stacks.

About stacks

LDM and **STM** are frequently used to store registers on, and retrieve them from, a stack. A stack is an area of memory which 'grows' in one direction as items are added to it, and 'shrinks' as they are taken off. Items are always removed from the stack in the reverse order to which they are added.

The term 'stack' comes from an analogy with stacks of plates that you see in self-service restaurants. Plates are added to the top, then removed in the opposite order. Another name for a stack is a last-in, first-out structure or 'LIFO'.

Computing stacks have a value associated with them called the stack pointer, or SP. The SP holds the address of the next item to be added to (pushed onto) or removed (pulled) from the stack. In an ARM program, the SP will almost invariably be stored in one of the general-purpose registers. Usually, a high-numbered register, e.g. R12 or R13 is used. The Acorn ARM Calling Standard, for example, specifies R12, whereas BASIC uses R13.

Here is a pictorial representation of two items being pushed onto a stack.

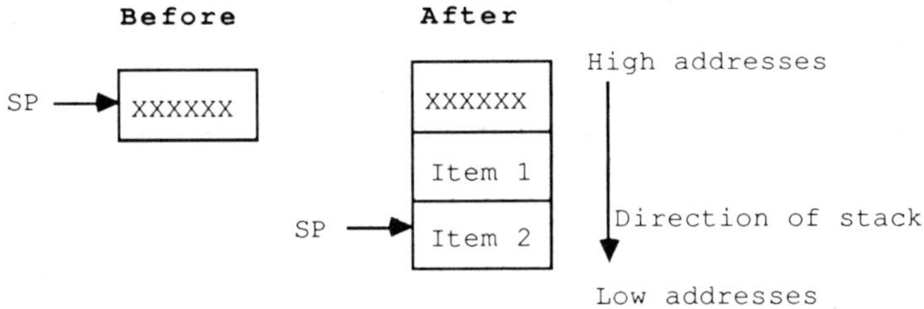

Before the items are pushed, SP points to (holds the address of) the previous item that was pushed. After two new words have been pushed, the stack pointer points to the second of these, and the first word pushed lies 'underneath' it.

Stacks on the ARM have two attributes which must be decided on before any **STM/LDM** instructions are used. The attributes must be used consistently in any further operation on the stack.

The first attribute is whether the stack is 'full' or 'empty'. A full stack is one in which the SP points to the last item pushed (like the example above). An empty stack is where the stack pointer holds the address of the empty slot where the *next* item will be pushed.

Secondly, a stack is said to be ascending or descending. An ascending stack is one where the SP is incremented when items are pushed and decremented when items are pulled. A descending stack grows and shrinks in the opposite direction. Given the direction of growth in the example above,the stack can be seen to be descending.

The above-mentioned Acorn Calling Standard (which defines the way in which separate programs may communicate) specifies a full, descending stack, and BASIC also uses one.

STM Store multiple registers

In the context of what has just been said, **STM** is the 'push items onto stack' instruction. Although it has other uses, most **STM**s are stack oriented.

The general form of the STM instruction is:

```
STM<type> <base>{!}, <registers>
```

We have omitted the **{cond}** for clarity, but as usual a condition code may be included immediately after the mnemonic. The **<type>** consists of two letters which determine the **F**ull/**E**mpty, **A**scending/**D**escending mode of the stack. The first letter is **F** or **E**; the second is **A** or **D**.

The **<base>** register is the stack pointer. As with **LDR/STR**, the **!** option will cause write-back if present. **<registers>** is a list of the registers which we want to push. It is specified as a list of register numbers separated by commas, enclosed in braces (curly brackets). You can also specify a list of registers using a - sign, e.g. **R0-R4** is shorthand for **R0,R1,R2,R3,R4**.

Our first example of an **STM** instruction is:

```
STMED   R13!,{R1,R2,R5}
```

This will save the three registers R1, R2 and R5 using R13 as the SP. As write-back is specified, R13 will be updated by subtracting 3*4 (12) from its original value (subtracting as we are using a descending stack). Because we have specified the **E** option, the stack is empty, i.e. after the **STM**, R13 will hold the address of the next word to be pushed. The address of the last word pushed is R13+4.

When using **STM** and **LDM** for stack operations, you will almost invariably use the **!** option, as the stack pointer has to be updated. Exceptions are when you want to obtain a copy of an item without pulling it, and when you need to store a result in a 'slot' which has been created for it on the stack. Both these techniques are used in the 'find substring' example of Chapter Six.

More on FD etc.

The ascending/descending mode of a stack is analogous to positive and negative offsets of the previous section. During an **STM**, if the stack is descending, a negative offset of 4 is used. If the stack is ascending, a positive offset of 4 is used (for each register).

Similarly, the difference between what the ARM does for full and empty stacks during an **STM** is analogous to the pre- and post-indexed addressing modes of the previous section. Consider a descending stack. An empty stack's pointer is post-decremented when an item is pushed. That is, the register to be pushed is stored at the current location, then the stack pointer is decremented (by a fixed offset of 4), ready for the next one. A full stack is pre-decremented on a push: first SP is decremented by 4, then the register is stored there. This is repeated for each register in the list.

Direction of storage

Below is an **STM** which stores all of the registers at the location pointed to by R13, but without affecting R13 (no write-back).

```
STMFD  R13,{R0-R15}
```

Although the stack is an **FD** one, because there is no write-back, R13 is not actually decremented. Thus after the operation, R13 points to some previous item, and below that in memory are the sixteen pushed words.

Now, as R0 appears first in the list, you might expect that to be the first register to be pushed, and to be stored at address R13-4. Well, you would be wrong. Firstly, the order in which the register list appears has no bearing at all on the order in which things are done. All the assembler is looking for is a mention of a register's name: it can appear anywhere within the braces. Secondly, the registers are always stored in the same order in memory, whether the stack is ascending or descending, full or empty.

When you push one or more registers, the ARM stores the lowest-numbered one at the lowest address, the next highest-numbered one at the next address and so on. This always occurs. For ascending stacks, the location pointer is updated, the first register stored (or vice versa for empty stacks) and so on for each register. Finally, if write-back is enabled, the stack pointer is updated by the location pointer.

For descending stacks, the final value of the stack pointer is calculated first. Then the registers are stored in increasing memory locations, and finally the stack pointer is updated if necessary.

We go into this detail because if you need to access pushed registers directly from the stack, it is important to know where they are!

Saving the stack pointer and PC

In the previous example, the stack pointer (R13) was one of the registers pushed. As there was no write-back, the value of R13 remained constant throughout the operation, so there is no question of what value was actually stored. However, in cases where write-back is enabled, the SP changes value at some time during the instruction, so the 'before' or 'after' version might be saved.

The rule which determines which version of the base register is saved is quite simple. If the stack pointer is the lowest-numbered one in the list, then the value stored is the original, unaltered one. Otherwise, the written-back value of the base register is that stored on the stack. Since we have standardised on R13 for the stack pointer, it is almost always the new value which is stored.

When R15 is included in the register list, all 32-bits are stored, i.e. both the PC and status register parts.

LDM Load multiple registers

LDM perform the stack 'pull' (or pop as it is also known) operation. It is very similar in form to the **STM** instruction:

```
LDM<type>  <base>{!},<registers>{^}
```

As before, the **<type>** gives the direction and type of the stack. When pulling registers, you must use the same type of stack as when they were pushed, otherwise the wrong values will be loaded. **<base>**, **!** and **<registers>** are all as **STM**.

The only extra 'twiddle' provided by **LDM** is the ^ which may appear at the end. If present, this indicates that if R15 is in the register list, then all 32-bits are to be updated from the value pulled from the stack. If there is no ^ in the instruction, then if R15 is pulled, only the PC portion (bits 2-25) are affected. The status bits of R15 will remain unaltered by the operation.

This enables you to decide whether subroutines (which are explained in detail in the next section) preserve the status flags or use them to return results. If you want the routine to preserve the flags, then use ^ to restore them from the stack. Otherwise omit it, and the flags will retain their previous contents.

Loading the stack pointer and PC

If the register being used as the stack pointer is in the **LDM** register list, the register's value after the instruction is always that which was loaded, irrespective of where it appeared in the list, and whether write-back was specified.

If R15 appears in the list, then the ^ option is used to determine whether the PC alone or PC plus status register is loaded. This is described above.

An alternative notation

Not all of the uses for **LDM** and **STM** involve stacks. In these situations, the full/empty, ascending/descending view of the operations may not be the most suitable. The assembler recognises an alternative set of option letters, which in fact mirrors more closely what the ARM instructions really do.

The alternative letter pairs are **I/D** for increment/decrement, and **B/A** for before/after. Thus the instruction:

```
STMIA   R0!,{R1,R2}
```

stores R1 and R2 at the address in R0. For each store, a post-increment (**I**ncrement **A**fter) is performed, and the new value (R0+8) is written back. Similarly:

```
LDMDA   R0!,{R1,R3,R4}
```

loads the three registers specified, decrementing the address after each one. The write-back option means that R0 will be decremented by 12. Remember that registers are always stored lowest at lowest address, so in terms of the original R0, the registers in the list will be loaded from addresses R0-8, R0-4 and R0-0 respectively.

The table below shows the equivalents for two types of notation:

Full/Empty	Decrement/Increment equivalent
STMFD	STMDB
LDMFD	LDMIA
STMFA	STMIB
LDMFA	LDMDA
STMED	STMDA
LDMED	LDMIB
STMEA	STMIA
LDMEA	LDMDB

The increment/decrement type notation shows how push and pull operations for a given type of stack are exact opposites.

Summary of LDM/STM

```
LDM{cond}<type1>  <base>{!},<registers>{^}
LDM{cond}<type2>  <base>{!},<registers>{^}
STM{cond}<type1>  <base>{!},<registers>{^}
STM{cond}<type2>  <base>{!},<registers>{^}
```

where:

cond is defined at the start of this chapter.
<type1> is **F|E A|D**
<type2> is **I|D B|A**
<base> is a register
<registers> is open-brace comma-separated-list close-brace

Notice that **^** may be used in **STM** as well as **LDM**. Its use in **STM** is only relevant to non-user modes, and as such is described in Chapter Seven.

3.5 Group four - branch

In theory, the group one data instructions could be used to make any change to the PC required by a program. For example, an **ADD** to R15 could be used to move the PC on by some amount, causing a jump forward in the program. However, there are limits to what you can achieve conveniently using these general-purpose instructions. The branch group provides the ability to locate any point in the program with a single operation.

The simple branch

Group four consists of just two variants of the branch instruction. There are (refreshingly perhaps) no alternative operand formats or optional extras. The basic instruction is a simple branch, whose mnemonic is just **B**. The format of the instruction is:

```
B{cond}    <expression>
```

The optional condition, when present, makes the mnemonic a more normal-looking three-letter one, e.g. **BNE**, **BCC**. If you prefer three letters, you could always express the unconditional branch as **BAL**, though the assembler would be happy with just **B**.

<expression> is the address within the program to which you wish to transfer control. Usually, it is just a label which is defined elsewhere in the program. For example, a simple counting loop would be implemented thus:

```
        MOV     R0,#0           ;Init the count to zero
.LOOP   MOVS    R1,R1,LSR#1     ;Get next 1 bit in Carry
        ADC     R0,#0           ;Add it to count
        BNE     LOOP            ;Loop if more to do
```

The 'program' counts the number of 1 bits in R1 by shifting them a bit at a time into the carry flag and adding the carry to R0. If the **MOV** left a non-zero result in R1, the branch causes the operation to repeat (note that the **ADC** doesn't affect the status as it has no **S** option).

Offsets and pipelining

When the assembler converts a branch instruction into the appropriate binary code, it calculates the offset from the current instruction to the destination address. The offset is encoded in the instruction word as a 24-bit word address, like the PC in R15. This is treated as a signed number, and when a branch is executed the offset is added to the current PC to reach the destination.

Calculation of the offset is a little more involved than you might at first suspect - once again due to pipelining. Suppose the location of a branch instruction is &1230, and the destination label is at address &1288. At first sight it appears the byte offset is &1288-&1230 = &58 bytes or &16 words. This is indeed the difference between the addresses. However, by the time the ARM gets round to executing an instruction, the PC has already moved two instructions further on.

Given the presence of pipelining, you can see that by the time the ARM starts to execute the branch at &1230, the PC contains &1238, i.e. the address of two instructions along. It is this address from which the offset to the destination must be calculated. To complete the example, the assembler adds &8 to &1230 to obtain &1238. It then subtracts this from the destination address of &1288 to obtain an offset of &50 bytes or &14 words, which is the number actually encoded in the instruction. Luckily you don't have to think about this when using the **B** instruction.

Branch with link

The single variant on the branch theme is the option to perform a link operation before the branch is executed. This simply means storing the current value of R15 in R14 before the branch is taken, so that the program has some way of returning there. Branch with link, **BL**, is used to implement subroutines, and replaces the more usual **BSR** (branch to subroutine) and **JSR** (jump to subroutine) instructions found on some computers.

Most processors implement **BSR** by saving the return address on the stack. Since ARM has no dedicated stack, it can't do this. Instead it copies R15 into R14. Then, if the called routine needs to use R14 for something, it can save it on the stack explicitly. The ARM method has the advantage that subroutines which don't need to save R14 can be called and return very quickly. The disadvantage is that all other routines have the overhead of explicitly saving R14.

The address that ARM saves in R14 is that of the instruction immediately following the **BL**. (Given pipelining, it should be the one after that, but the processor automatically adjusts the value saved.) So, to return from a subroutine, the program simply has to move R14 back into R15:

```
MOVS    R15,R14
```

The version shown will restore the original flags too, automatically making the subroutine preserve them. If some result was to be passed back in the status register, a **MOV** without **S** could be used. This would only transfer the PC portion of R14 back to R15, enabling the subroutine to pass status information back in the flags.

BL has the expected format:

```
BL{cond}    <expression>
```

3.6 Group five - software interrupt

The final group is the most simple, and the most complex. It is very simple because it contains just one instruction, **SWI**, whose assembler format has absolutely no variants or options.

The general form of **SWI** is:

```
SWI{cond}  <expression>
```

It is complex because depending on **<expression>**, **SWI** will perform tasks as disparate as displaying characters on the screen, setting the auto-repeat speed of the keyboard and loading a file from the disc.

SWI is the user's access to the operating system of the computer. When a **SWI** is executed, the CPU enters supervisor mode, saves the return address in R14_SVC, and jumps to location 8. From here, the operating system takes over. The way in which the **SWI** is used depends on **<expression>**. This is encoded as a 24-bit field in the instruction. The operating system can examine the instruction using, for example:.

```
STMFD   R13!,{R0-R12}          ;Save user's registers
BIC     R14,R14,#&FC000003     ;Mask status bits
LDR     R13,[R14,#-4]          ;Load SWI instruction
```

to find out what **<expression>** is.

Since the interpretation of **<expression>** depends entirely on the system in which the program is executing, we cannot say much more about **SWI** here. However, as practical programs need to use operating system functions, the examples in later chapters will use a 'standard' set that you could reasonably expect. Two of the most important ones are called **WriteC** and **ReadC**. The former sends the character in the bottom byte of R0 to the screen, and the latter reads a character from the keyboard and returns it in the bottom byte of R0.

Note: The code in the example above will be executed in **SVC** mode, so the accesses to R13 and R14 are actually to R13_SVC and R14_SVC. Thus the user's versions of these registers do not have to be saved.

3.7 Instruction timings

It is informative to know how quickly you can expect instructions to execute. This section gives the timing of all of the ARM instructions. The times are expressed in terms of 'cycles'. A cycle is one tick of the crystal oscillator clock which drives the ARM. In fact there are three types of cycles, called sequential, non-sequential and internal.

Sequential (s) cycles are those used to access memory locations in sequential order. For example, when the ARM is executing a series of group one instructions with no interruption from branches and load/store operations, sequential cycles will be used.

Non-sequential (n) cycles are those used to access external memory when non-consecutive locations are required. For example, the first instruction to be loaded after a branch instruction will use an n-cycle.

Internal (i) cycles are those used when the ARM is not accessing memory at all, but performing some internal operation.

On a typical ARM, the clock speed is 8MHz (eight million cycles a second). S cycles last 125 nanoseconds for RAM and 250ns for ROM. All n-cycles are 250ns. All i-cycles are 125ns in duration.

Instructions which are skipped due to the condition failing always execute in 1s cycle.

Group one

MOV, ADD etc. 1 s-cycle. If **<rhs>** contains a shift count in a register (i.e. not an immediate shift), add 1 s-cycle. If **<dest>** is R15, add 1 s + 1 n-cycle.

Group one A

MUL, MLA. 1 s + 16 i- cycles worst-case.

Group two

LDR. 1 s + 1 n + 1 i-cycle. If **<dest>** is R15, add 1 s + 1n-cycle.

STR. 2 n-cycles.

Group three

LDM. (regs-1) s + 1 n + 1 i-cycle. Regs is the number of registers loaded. Add 1 s + 1 n-cycles if R15 is loaded.

STM. 2 n + (regs-1) s-cycles.

Group four

B, BL. 2 s + 1 n-cycles.

Group five

SWI. 2 s + 1 n-cycles.

From these timings you can see that when the ARM executes several group one instructions in sequence, it does so at a rate of eight million a second. The overhead of calling and returning from a subroutine is 3 s+1 n-cycles, or 0.525 microseconds if the return address is stored, or 2 s+5 n-cycles, or 1.5µs if the return address is stacked.

A multiply by zero or one takes 125ns. A worst-case multiply takes 2.125µs. Saving eight registers on the stack takes 7 s + 2 n-cycles, or 1.375µs. Loading them back, if one of them is the PC, takes 1.75 µ6s.

4. The BBC BASIC assembler

There are two main ways of writing ARM assembly language programs. One is to use a dedicated assembler. Such a program takes a text file containing ARM assembly language instructions, assembles it, and produces another file containing the equivalent machine code. These two files are called the source files and object files respectively.

An alternative approach is to use the assembler built-in to BBC BASIC. The ability to mix assembler with BASIC is a very useful feature of the language, and one that is relatively straightforward to use. For this reason, and because of the widespread availability of BBC BASIC, we describe how to use its built-in assembler. The examples of the next two chapters are also in the format expected by the BASIC assembler.

4.1 First principles

Two special 'statements' are used to enter and exit from the assembler. The open square bracket character, `[`, marks the start of assembly language source. Whenever this character is encountered where BASIC expects to see a statement like **`PRINT`** or an assignment, BASIC stops executing the program and starts to assemble ARM instructions into machine code. The end of the source is marked by the close square bracket, `]`. If this is read where BASIC is expecting to see an instruction to be assembled, it leaves assembler mode and starts executing the (BASIC) program again.

To see the effect of entering and leaving the assembler, type in this short program:

```
10 PRINT "Outside the assembler"
20 [ ;In the assembler
30 ]
40 PRINT "Outside the assembler"
```

If you RUN this, you should see something like the following:

```
Outside the assembler
00000000                  ;In the assembler
Outside the assembler
```

Between the two lines produced by the **PRINT** statements is one which the assembler printed. Unless you tell it not to, the assembler prints an assembly listing. We shall describe this in detail, but for now suffice is to say that it consists of three parts: an address (the eight zeros above, which may be different when *you* run the program), the machine code instruction in hex, and the source instruction being assembled.

In our example above, no instructions were assembled, so no machine code was listed. The only line of source was a comment. The semi-colon, ;, introduces a line of comment to the assembler. This acts much as a **REM** in BASIC, and causes the text after it to be ignored. The comment was indented somewhat in the assembly listing, as the assembler leaves space for any machine code which might be produced.

The address printed at the start of the line is called the location counter. This tells us two things: where the assembler is placing assembled machine code instructions in memory, and what the value of the program counter (PC) will be when that instruction is fetched for execution, when the program finally comes to be run. Because we are not assembling any instructions, no code will be written to memory, so it doesn't matter what the location counter's value is. Normally, though, when you assemble code, you should set the location counter to some address where the assembler may store the machine code.

It is easy to set the location counter, as it is stored in the system integer variable P%. If you enter the immediate statement:

```
PRINT  ~P%
```

you will see the same figures printed as at the start of the middle line above (except for leading zeros).

Let us now assemble some actual code. To do this, we need to reserve some storage for the object code. This is easily done using the form of **DIM** which reserves a given number of bytes. Type in the following:

```
10  DIM  org  40
20  P%  =  org
30  [  ;A  simple  ARM  program
40  MOV  R0,#32
50.LOOP
60  SWI  0
70  ADD  R0,R0,#1
80  CMP  R0,#126
90  BNE  LOOP
100  MOV  R15,R14
110  ]
```

It may seem strange using the variable **org** in the **DIM**, then using it only once to set P%, but we shall see the reason for this later. Note that the **DIM** statement returns an address which is guaranteed to be aligned on a word boundary, so there is no need to 'force' it to be a multiple of four.

As in the previous example, the first line of the assembler is a comment. The next seven lines though are actual assembly language instructions. In fact, you may recognise the program as being very similar to the example given at the end of Chapter One. It is a simple loop, which prints the character set from ASCII 32 (space) to ASCII 126 (tilde or ~).

The lines which are indented by a space are ARM mnemonics, followed by their operands. When the assembler encounters these, it will convert the instruction into the appropriate four-byte machine code, and then store this at the current location counter - P%. Then P% will be increased by four for the next instruction.

Line 50, which starts with a `.`, is a label. A label is a variable which marks the current place in the program. When it encounters a label, the assembler stores the current value of the location counter into the variable, so that this place in the program may be accessed in a later instruction. In this case the **BNE** at line 90 uses the label **LOOP** to branch back to the **SWI** instruction. Any numeric variable may be used as a label, but by convention floating point variables (without % sign) are used. Every label in a program should have a unique name. This isn't hard to achieve as BBC BASIC allows very long names.

If you RUN the program, another assembly listing will be produced, this time looking like:

```
000167C8                           ;A  simple  ARM  program
000167C8  E3A00020                 MOV  R0,#32
000167CC            .LOOP
000167CC  EF000000                 SWI  0
000167D0  E2800001                 ADD  R0,R0,#1
000167D4  E350007E                 CMP  R0,#126
000167D8  1AFFFFFB                 BNE  LOOP
000167DC  E1A0F00E                 MOV  R15,R14
```

The first column is the location counter, and in the listing above, we can see that the first machine instruction was placed at address &167C8. Next is the hex representation of that instruction, i.e. the code which will actually be fetched and executed by the processor. You can verify that this is what was stored by the assembler by typing in:

```
PRINT  ~!&167C8
```

(The address should be whatever was printed when you ran the program.) You will see **E3A00020**, as in the listing.

In the third column is the label for that instruction, or spaces if there isn't one, followed by the rest of the line, as typed by you.

To see the fruits of you labours, type the command:

```
CALL  org
```

The ASCII character set of the machine will be printed. The **CALL** statement takes the address of a machine code routine, which it then executes. The machine code is called as if a **BL** instruction had been used with the address given as the operand. Thus to return to BASIC, the return address in R14 is transferred to R15 (the PC) as in the example above.

We will have more to say about using **CALL** (and the associated function **USR**) later in this chapter.

4.2 Passes and assembly options

Frequently, a label is defined *after* the place (or places) in the program from which it is used. For example, a forward branch might have this form:

```
100  CMP  R0,#10
110  BNE  notTen
120  ;  some  instructions
130  ;  ...
140.notTen
```

In this example, the label **notTen** has not been encountered when the instruction at line 110 is assembled. It is not defined until line 140. If this or a similar sequence of instructions were encountered while assembling a program using the method we have already described, a message of the type '**Unknown or missing variable**' would be produced.

We clearly need to be able to assemble programs with forward references, and the BBC BASIC assembler adopts the same approach to the problem as many others: it makes two scans, or passes, over the program. The first one is to enable all the labels to be defined, and the second pass assembles the code proper.

In the BASIC assembler we tell it to suppress 'errors' during the first pass by using the **OPT** directive. A directive (or pseudo-op as they are also called) is an instruction which doesn't get converted into machine code, but instead instructs the assembler to perform some action. It is used in the same place as a proper instruction.

The **OPT** directive is followed by a number, and is usually placed immediately after the **[**, but can in fact be used anywhere in the source code. The number is interpreted as a three-bit value. Bit zero controls the assembly listing; bit one controls whether '**Unknown or missing variable**' type errors are suppressed or not, and bit two controls something called offset assembly, which we shall come to later. The eight possible values may be summarised as below:

Value	Offset assembly	Errors given	Listing
0	No	No	No
1	No	No	Yes
2	No	Yes	No
3	No	Yes	Yes
4	Yes	No	No
5	Yes	No	Yes
6	Yes	Yes	No
7	Yes	Yes	Yes

If you don't use **OPT** at all, the default state is 3 - offset assembly is not used; errors are not suppressed, and a listing is given.

The most obvious way to obtain the two passes in BASIC is to enclose the whole of the source code in a **FOR...NEXT** loop which performs two iterations. Often, the code is enclosed in a procedure so that the **FOR** and **NEXT** of the loop can be close together. The desired assembly option can then be passed as a parameter to the procedure.

Below is an example following the outline described above. The program contains a forward reference to illustrate the use of two passes. The listing is produced in the second pass (as it always should be if there are two passes), so the values given to **OPT** are 0 and 3 respectively.

```
1000  REM Example of two-pass assembly
1010  DIM org 100
1030  FOR pass=0 TO 3 STEP 3
1040      PROCasm(pass,org)
1050  NEXT pass
1060  END
1070
2000  DEF  PROCasm(pass,org)
2010  P%=org
2020  [ OPT pass
2030  .loop
2040  SWI    4          ;Read a char
2050  MOVS   R0,R0,ASR#1
```

```
2055  MOVEQ   R15, R14
2060  BCC     even
2070  SWI     256+ASC"O" ;Print O
2080  B       loop
2090  .even
2100  SWI     256+ASC"E" ;Print E
2110  B       loop
2120  ]
2130  ENDPROC
```

The most important thing to notice is that the P% variable is set at the start of each pass. If you only set it at the start of the first pass, by the end of the first pass it will contain the address of the end of the code, and be incorrect for the start of the second pass.

The program is fairly trivial. It reads characters from the keyboard and prints **E** if the character has an even ASCII code, or **O** if not. This repeats until an ASCII character 0 or 1 (**CTRL @** or **CTRL A**) is typed. The branch to **even** at line 2060 is a forward one; during the first pass the fact that **even** hasn't been defined yet is ignored, then during the second pass, its value - set in line 2090 - is used to address the following **SWI**.

In fact, because of the ARM's conditional instructions, this program could have been written without any forward branches, by making lines 2070 and 2080:

```
2070 SWICS    256+"O";Print O
2080 SWICC    256+"E";Print E
```

and deleting lines 2090 and 2100. It's always hard thinking of simple but useful ways of illustrating specific points.

You should be aware of what actually happens when a forward reference is encountered in the first pass. Instead of giving an error, the assembler uses the current value of the location counter. In line 2060 above, for example, the value returned for the undefined variable is the address of the **BCC** instruction itself. If only the first pass was performed and you tried to call the code, an infinite loop would be caused by this branch to itself. It is important, therefore, that you always set bit 1 of the **OPT** value during the second pass, to enable errors to be reported, even if you don't bother about the listing.

4.3 Program style and readability

Any experienced assembler language programmer reading this chapter will probably be thinking by now, 'What a load of rubbish.' The examples presented so far are not, it must be admitted, models of clarity and elegance.

This was deliberate; it gives us a chance to point out how they are deficient and how these deficiencies may be remedied.

As we learned in Chapter One, assembly language is about as far from the ideal as a normal human programmer is likely to venture. When writing an assembly language program, you should therefore give your reader as much help as possible in understanding what is going on. Bear in mind that the reader may well be you, so it's not just a question of helping others.

Comments are the first line of attack. As we have seen, comments may appear as the first (and only) thing on the line, or after the label, or after the label and instruction. A comment may not come between the label and instruction, as the instruction will be ignored, being taken as part of the comment. We have used ; to introduce comments, as this is the same character that many other assemblers use. The BBC BASIC assembler also allows you to use \ and **REM**. Whatever you use, you should be consistent.

A comment should be meaningful. The comments at the start of a routine should explain what it does, what the entry and exit conditions are, and what the side-effects are. Entry and exit conditions usually pertain to the contents of the ARM registers when the routine is called and when it returns, but may also include the state of specific memory locations at these points too.

The side-effects of a routine are similar to saying what it does, but are more concerned with actions which might affect the operation of other routines. A common side-effect is that of corrupting certain registers. Another example might be a routine which prints a character on the screen as its main action, but corrupts a pointer in RAM as a side-effect. By documenting these things in comments, you make it much easier to track down bugs, and to interface your routines to each other.

From the remarks above, it can be seen that the routines presented above are poorly served with comments, and this makes it more difficult to understand them, even though they are quite short.

Another important way of increasing readability is to use names instead of numbers. Examples where this clouded the issue in earlier programs are:

```
  80 CMP   R0,#126

2040 SWI   4    ;Read a char
```

Admittedly the second example has a comment which gives the reader some idea, but the first one is totally meaningless to many people. In the BBC BASIC assembler, wherever a number is required in an operand, the full power of the BASIC expression evaluator is available. The most obvious way to utilise this is to use variables as names for 'magic' numbers. For example, in the character program, we could have included an assignment

```
17 maxChar = ASC"~"
```

and made line 80:

```
80 CMP   R0,  #maxChar
```

In the first place we are told in line 17 what the last character to be printed is, and secondly the name **maxChar** gives a much better indication in line 80 of what we are comparing.

In the second example, the operand to **SWI** was a code number telling the operating system what routine was desired. This was the read character routine which goes by the name of **ReadC**. So the program can be made more readable by adding the line:

```
1005 ReadC = 4  : REM SWI to read a char into R0
```

and changing line 2040 to:

```
2040 SWI ReadC
```

which makes the comment redundant. The **SWI 256** is another instruction that can be improved. This particular **SWI** has an operand of the form 256+ch, where ch is the code of character to be printed. It is given the name **WriteI** (for write immediate) in Acorn documentation, so we could have an assignment like this:

```
1007 WriteI=&100  : REM SWI to write char in LSB of operand
```

and change the instructions to have the form:

```
2070 SWI WriteI+ASC"O"
```

The importance of giving names to things like **SWI** codes and immediate operands cannot be understated. A similarly useful tool is naming registers. So far we have used the denotations R0, R1 etc. to stand for registers. In addition to these standard names, the assembler accepts an expression which evaluates to a register number. An obvious application of this is to give names to important registers such as the SP by assigning the appropriate register number to a variable. For example, if we had these three assignments in the BASIC part of a program:

```
10 link = 14     : REM BL link register
20 sp = 13       : REM My stack pointer register
30 acc = 5       : REM Accumulator for results
```

then instructions could take the form:

```
1000  MOVCS   pc,link             ;Return if too big
1210  STM     (sp)!,{acc,link}    ;Save result and return addr
2300  LDM     (sp)!,{acc,pc}      ;Return and restore
```

There are two things to note about these examples. The first is that we use the name **pc** even though this wan't one of the variables we defined above. The BASIC assembler recognises it automatically and substitutes **R15**. The second is that **sp** has brackets around it. These are required because the **!** sign is used by BASIC to denote 'indirection'. To stop BASIC from getting confused you have to put brackets around any variable name used before a **!** in **STM** and **LDM** instructions. You don't need the brackets if a register name, such as **R13**, is used.

In the examples in this book, we use the names **pc**, **link** and **sp** as shown above, and we also use names for other registers where possible. There is no confusion between register numbers and immediate operands, of course, because the latter are preceded by a **#** sign. So:

```
4310  MOV  acc,sp
```

copies the contents of register **sp** (i.e. R13) to register **acc**, whereas:

```
4310  MOV  acc,#sp
```

would load the immediate value 13 into the **acc** register.

The final point about style concerns layout. The assembler doesn't impose too many constraints on the way in which you lay out the program. As we have already mentioned, labels must come immediately after the line number, and comments must appear as the last (and possibly only) thing on the line. However, it is advisable to line up the columns where possible. This makes it easier to follows comments if nothing else. Comments describing individual routines or the whole program can be placed at the start of the line. This also applies to comments for instructions which wouldn't fit on the line easily (e.g. after an **STR** with a long register list).

Line spacing can also be important. It is a good idea to leave blank lines between routines to separate them.

A typical format would be: ten spaces for the label, 25 for the instruction, and the rest of the line for the comment. For example:

```
1230           MOV  count, #15       ;Init the counter
1240.loop      SWI  writeI+ASC"*"    ;Print an asterisk
1250           SUB  count, #1        ;Next count
1260           BNE  loop
```

Another minor point of style in the listing above is the spacing of operands. It is easier to separate operands if there is at least one space character between them.

By way of a simple contrast, we list the very first program of this chapter, trying to practise that which we have just been preaching.

```
 10 DIM org 40
 20 P% = org
 30 outReg = 0 : REM Register use by WriteC. Preserved
 40 link =   14 : REM BL link register
 50 pc   =   15 : REM ARM program counter
 60 WriteC = 0 : REM SWI code to print char in R0
 70 firstChar = ASC" "
 80 lastChar = ASC"~"
 90 [
100 ;A simple ARM program. This prints the ASCII
110 ;character set from 'firstChar' to 'lastChar'
120 MOV  outReg, #firstChar         ;Init the output char
130.loop
140 SWI  WriteC                     ;Display the char.
150 ADD  outReg, outReg, #1         ;Increment the character
160 CMP  outReg, #lastChar          ;Finished?
170 BNE  loop                       ;No so loop
180 MOV  pc, link                   ;else return
190 ]
```

Because the line numbers are not particularly relevant to the assembly language, listings in subsequent chapters don't use them.

Finally, a note on cases. The assembler is totally case-insensitive. Mnemonics and 'R's in R0 etc. may be in upper or lower case or any combination thereof. Labels, however, must obey the rules of the rest of BASIC, which state that variable names are case dependent. Thus **LOOP** is a different label from **loop**, and **Loop** is again different. The convention used in this book is upper case for mnemonics and R0-type designations, and a mixture of upper and lower case (e.g. **strPtr**) for labels and other names. As usual, the method you adopt is up to you, consistency being the important thing.

4.4 Offset assembly

The facility of offset assembly was mentioned above. It is enabled by bit 2 of the **OPT** expression. When offset assembly is used, the code is still assembled to execute at the address in the P% variable. However, it is not stored there. Instead, it is placed at the address held in the O% variable.

Motivation for offset assembly can be explained as follows. Suppose you are writing a program which will load and execute at address &8000. Now, using **DIM** to obtain code space, you find you can only obtain addresses from about &8700 up. You could set P% explicitly to &8000, but as this is where the BASIC interpreter's workspace lies, you will be in dire danger of overwriting it. This invariably leads to unpleasantness.

The solution to this dilemma is to still assign P% to &8000, as if it is going to execute there, but use offset assembly to store the machine code at some conveniently **DIM**med location. Here is the outline of a program using offset assembly, without line numbers.

```
org = &1000     : REM Where we want the code to run
DIM code 500    : REM Where the code is assembled to
code$= "  "+STR$~code+"  "
org$ = "  "+STR$~org+"  "

FOR pass=4 TO 6 STEP 2
    P%=org
    O%=code
    [   OPT pass
    ;The lines of the program come here
    ;...
    ;...
    ]
NEXT pass
OSCLI "SAVE PROG "+code$+STR$~O%+org$+org$
```

Both P% and O% are set at the start of each pass. Because bit 2 of the pass looping value is set, offset assembly will take place and the assembled code will actually be stored from the address in **code**. Once assembled, the code is saved with the appropriate load and execution addresses, and could be activated using a * command.

When using offset assembly, you shouldn't use **CALL** to test the machine code, as it will be assembled to execute at an address different from the one in which it is stored.

Having illustrated the use of offset assembly, we will now say that you should rarely have to use it. As the next chapter tries to show, it is quite easy to write ARM programs which operate correctly at any load address. Such programs are called position independent, and there are a few simple rules you have to obey in order to give your programs this desirable property.

Overleaf is a version of the outline listing above, assuming that the program between the [and] statements is position independent.

```
org = &1000    : REM Where we want the code to run
DIM code 500   : REM Where the code is assembled to
code$= "  "+STR$~code+"  "
org$ = "  "+STR$~org+"  "

FOR pass=0 TO 2 STEP 2
    P%=code
    [   OPT pass
    ;The lines of the program come here
    ;...
    ;...
    ]
NEXT pass
OSCLI "SAVE PROG "+code$+STR$~P%+org$+org$
```

The differences are that O% doesn't get a mention, and the values for the **OPT** directive are 0 and 2 respectively. The value of **org** is used only to set the load and execution addresses in the **SAVE** command.

In the light of the above, you may be wondering why offset assembly is allowed at all. It is really a carry-over from early versions of BBC BASIC, running on the BBC Micro. These incorporated assemblers for the old-fashioned 6502 processor that the BBC machine used. It is virtually impossible to write position independent code for the 6502, so offset assembly was very useful, especially for those writing 'paged ROM' software.

There is still one valid use for offset assembly, and that is in defining areas of memory for data storage. We shall describe this in the next section.

4.5 Defining space

Most programs need some associated data storage area. This might be used for constant data, such as tables of commands, or for holding items such as character strings (filenames etc.) or arrays of numbers which won't fit in the ARM's registers. There are four assembler directives which enable you to reserve space in the program for data. They are called:

EQUB - Reserve a byte
EQUW - Reserve a word (two bytes)
EQUD - Reserve a double word (four bytes)
EQUS - Reserve a string (0 to 255 bytes)

The reference to a 'word' being two bytes may be confusing in the light of our earlier claims that the ARM has a 32-bit or four-byte word length. Like offset assembly, the notation has its origins in the murky history of BBC BASIC. It's probably best to forget what the letters stand for, and just remember how many bytes each directive reserves.

Each of the directives is followed by an expression, an integer in the first three cases, and a string in the last. The assembler embeds the appropriate number of bytes into the machine code, and increments P% (and if necessary O%) by the right amount.

Here is an example of using EQUB. Suppose we are writing a VDU driver where control characters (in the range 0..31) may be followed by 1 or more 'parameter' bytes. We would require a table which, for each code, gave us the parameter count. This could be set-up using **EQUB** as below:

```
.parmCount
  ; This table holds the number of parameters bytes
  ; for the control codes in the range 0..31
 EQUB 0         ;NUL.  Zero parameters
 EQUB 1         ;To Printer.  One parm.
 EQUB 0         ;Printer on.  Zero parms.
 EQUB 0         ;Printer off.  Zero parms
 ....       ....
 ....       ....
 EQUB 4         ;Graf origin.  Four bytes
 EQUB 0         ;Home.  No parameters
 EQUB 2         ;Tab(x,y).  Two parms.
  ; End of parmCount table
  ;
```

Each of the **EQUB**s embeds the count byte given as the operand into the machine code. Then P% is moved on by one. In the case of **EQUW**, the two LSBs of the argument are stored (lowest byte first) and P% incremented by two. For **EQUD**, all four bytes of the integer operand are stored in standard ARM order (lowest byte to highest byte) and P% is incremented by 4.

There are a couple of points to note. We are storing data in the object code, not instructions. Therefore you have to ensure that the program will not try to 'execute' the bytes embedded by **EQUB** etc. For example, if there was code immediately before the label **parmCount** above, there should be no way for the code to 'drop through' into the data area. The result of executing data is unpredictable, but invariably nasty. For this reason it is wise to separate 'code' and 'data' sections of the program as much as possible.

Secondly, in the example above we embedded 32 bytes, which is a multiple of four. So assuming that P% started off on a word boundary, it would end up on one after the list of **EQUB**s. This means that if we started to assemble instructions after the table, there would be no problem. Suppose, however, that we actually embedded 33 bytes. After this, P% would no longer lie on a word boundary, and if we wanted to start to assemble instructions after the table, some corrective action would have to be taken. The **ALIGN** directive is used to perform this.

You can use **ALIGN** anywhere that an instruction can be used. Its effect is to force P% and O% to move on to the next word boundary. If they already are word-aligned, they are not altered. Otherwise, they are incremented by 1, 2 or 3 as appropriate, so that the new values are multiples of four.

The string directive, **EQUS**, enables us to embed a sequence of bytes represented by a BBC BASIC string into memory. For example, suppose we had a table of command names to embed in a program. Each name is terminated by having the top bit of its last letter set. We could set-up such a table like this:

```
.commands
 ; Table of commands.  Each command has the top bit
 ; of its last char.  set.  The table is terminated
 ; by a zero byte.
          EQUS  "ACCES"+CHR$(ASC"S"+&80)
          EQUS  "BACKU"+CHR$(ASC"P"+&80)
          EQUS  "COMPAC"+CHR$(ASC"T"+&80)
 ....
 ....
          EQUS  "TITL"+CHR$(ASC"E"+&80)
          EQUS  "WIP"+CHR$(ASC"E"+&80)
 ;
          EQUB  0
          ALIGN
 ; End of command table
```

Note the use of the **ALIGN** directive at the end of the table.

The examples presented so far have shown initialised memory being set-up, that is memory which contains read-only data for use by the program. The need to reserve space for initialised memory also arises. For example, say a program uses an operating system routine to load a file. This routine might require a parameter block in memory, which contains all of the data necessary to perform the load. To reserve space for the parameter block, a sequence of **EQUD**s could be used:

```
.fileBlock
 ; This is the parameter block for the file load operation
 ;
.namePtr     EQUD 0    ; Pointer to the filename
.loadAddr    EQUD 0    ; The load address of the file
.execAddr    EQUD 0    ; The execution address
.attributes  EQUD 0    ; The file's attributes
 ;
```

```
;
.doLoad
 ; This routine sets up the file block and loads the file
 ; It assumes the name is on the stack
 ;
        STR   sp, namePtr      ; Save the name pointer
        MOV   R0, #&1000       ; Get 4K for the file
        SWI   getMemory        ; Returns pointer in R1
        STR   R1, loadAddr     ; Save the address
 ; Get the address of the parameter block in R0
        ADR   R0, fileBlock
        MOV   R1, #loadCode    ; Command code for SWI
        SWI   file             ; Do the load
 ...
```

The **EQUD**s to set up the parameter block do not have meaningful operands. This is because they are only being used to reserve memory which will be later filled in by the program. Each **EQUD** has a label so that the address of the four-byte area reserved can be accessed by name.

Following the set-up directives is some code which would use such a parameter block. It uses some hypothetical **SWI** calls to access operating system routines, but you can assume that similar facilities will be available on any ARM system you are likely to use. Some of the instructions may not be very clear at this stage, but you might like to come back and re-examine the example having read the next two chapters.

The **ADR** instruction isn't an ARM mnemonic, but is a directive used to load a register with an address. The first operand is the register in which the address is to be stored. The second operand is the address to be loaded. The directive is converted into one of these instructions:

```
ADD  reg,pc,#addr-(P%+8)  or
SUB  reg,pc,#(P%+8)-addr
```

The first form is used if the **addr** is after the directive in the program, and the second form is used if **addr** appears earlier, as in the example above. The idea of using the directive is to obtain the required address in a position-independent manner, i.e. in a way which will work no matter where the program is executing. We say more about position-independence in Chapter Five.

To reserve space for items larger than double words, you can use **EQUS**. The operand should be a string whose length is the required number of bytes. The BASIC **STRING$** function provides a good way of obtaining such a string. The example below reserves two 32-byte areas:

```
.path1      EQUS  STRING$(32,CHR$0)   ;32 bytes for filename1
.path2      EQUS  STRING$(32,CHR$0)   ;32 bytes for filename2
```

By making the second operand of **STRING$ CHR$0**, the bytes embedded will by ASCII 0. As this is an illegal filename character, it can be used to guard against the program omitting to initialise the strings before using them.

In each of the examples above, the directives were used to reserve storage inside the machine code of the assembly language program. Another use is in defining labels as offsets from the start of some work area. For example, we may use register R10 as a pointer to a block of memory where we store important, frequently accessed data (but which doesn't fit in the registers). The **LDR** group of instructions would be used to access the data, using immediate offsets. Suppose the structure of the data is thus:

Offset	Item	Bytes
00	Program pointer	4
04	Top of program	4
08	Start of variables	4
12	End of variables	4
16	Character count	4
20	ON ERROR pointer	4
24	String length	1
25	List option	1
26	OPT value	1
27	....	1

The data items are the sort of thing that a BASIC interpreter would store in its data area. Notice that all of the word-length items are stored in one group so that they remain word aligned. One way of assigning the offsets in the BBC BASIC assembler would be with assignments:

```
page = 0
top = page+4
lomem = top+4
vartop = lomem+4
count = vartop+4
errptr = count+4
strlen = errptr+4
listo = strlen+1
opt = listo+1
....= opt+1
```

This method has a couple of drawbacks. First, to find out how many bytes have been allocated to a given item, you have to look at two lines and perform a subtraction. Similarly, to insert a new item, two lines have to be amended. Even worse, the actual values assigned to the labels can't be discovered without printing them individually - they don't appear in the assembly listing.

To overcome these drawbacks, we use the assembler's offset assembly ability. The method is illustrated below:

```
DIM org 1000  : REM Enough for code and data declarations
FOR pass=0 TO 2 STEP 2
  PROCdeclarations(org,pass)
  PROCasm(org,pass)
NEXT
END

 DEF  PROCdeclarations(org,pass)
 P%=0  :  O%=org
 [          OPT pass + 4
.page       EQUD  0
.top        EQUD  0
.lomem      EQUD  0
.vartop     EQUD  0
.count      EQUD  0
.errptr     EQUD  0
.strlen     EQUB  0
.listo      EQUB  0
.opt        EQUB  0
...         EQUB  0
 ]
 ENDPROC

 DEF  PROCasm(org,pass)
 P%=org
 [          OPT pass
 ....
```

The procedure **PROCdeclarations** contains the **EQU** directives which define the space for each item. By adding 4 to the **pass** value, offset assembly is used. Setting P% to zero means that the first label, **page**, will have the value zero; **top** will be set to 4, and so on. O% is set to **org** originally so that the bytes assembled by the directives will be stored in the same place as the program code. As **PROCasm** is called after **PROCdeclarations**, the code will overwrite the zero bytes.

When this technique is used, the addresses of the labels appear in the assembly listing (using **FOR pass=0 TO 3 STEP 3**); it is easier to see how many bytes each item occupies (by seeing which directive is used), and adding a new item is simply a matter of inserting the appropriate line.

4.6 Macros and conditional assembly

Sometimes, a sequence of instructions occurs frequently throughout a program. An example is setting up a table. Suppose we have a table which consists of 32 entries, each containing a branch instruction and three items of data, a two byte one and two single byte items. To set up the table, we could have a list of 32 instruction sequences, each of the form:

```
        B       address
        EQUW    data1
        EQUB    data2
        EQUB    data3
```

Typing in these four lines 32 times might prove a little laborious, and possibly error-prone.

Many dedicated assemblers provide a facility called *macros* to make life a little easier in situations like the one described above. A macro can be viewed as a template which is defined just once for the sequence. It is then 'invoked' using a single-line instruction to generate all of the instructions. The BBC BASIC assembler implements macros in a novel way, using the user-defined function keyword, **FN**.

If the assembler encounters an **FN** where it is expecting to find a mnemonic, the function is called as usual, but any result it returns is disregarded. Once you are in **FN**, you have the whole power of BASIC available. This includes the assembler, so you can start to assemble code within the **FN**. This will be added to the machine code which was already assembled in the main program.

To clarify the situation, we will implement a macro to make a table entry of the type described above.

```
10000  DEF  FNtable(address,data1,data2,data3)
10010 [          OPT          pass
10020            B            address
10030            EQUW         data1
10040            EQUB         data2
10050            EQUB         data3
10060  ]
10070  =""
```

As you can see, the 'body' of the macro is very similar to the list of instructions given earlier. The macro is defined in a separate part of the program, outside of the main assembly language section (hence the very high line number). It assumes that the looping variable used to control the passes of the assembler is called **pass**, but this could have been given as an extra parameter.

To call the macro, an **FNtable** call is used, one for each entry in the table. A typical sequence might look like this:

```
1240        FNtable(list,1,2,3)
1250        FNtable(delete,2,3,4)
1260        FNtable(renumber,1,1,2)
1270 ....
```

When the **FN** is reached, the assembler calls the function using the parameters supplied. The effect of this is to assemble the instructions and then return. The return value "" is disregarded. The net effect of all this is to assemble four lines of code with only one instruction.

Another use of macros is to 'invent' new instructions. For example, instead of always having to remember which type of stack you are using (full, empty, ascending or descending), you could define a macro which pushes a given range of registers. By always using the macro, you also avoid the pitfuls of forgetting the **!** to denote write-back.

The routine below is a macro to push a range of registers onto a full, descending stack, using R13.

```
10000 DEF  FNpush(first,last)
10010 [              OPT       pass
10020                STMFD     R13!,{first-last}
10030 ]
10040 =""
```

Another advantage of using a macro to implement a common operation like push is that it can be changed just the once to affect all of the places where it is used. Suppose, for example, that you have to change your program to use an empty stack, so that it is compatible with someone else's program. By simply changing line 10020 above, every push operation will use the new type of stack.

There are situations where you might want to be able to assemble different versions of a program, depending on some condition. This is where conditional assembly comes in.

Using conditional assembly is a bit like **IF**... type operations in BASIC, and that is exactly what we use to implement it in the BBC BASIC assembler. The listing overleaf shows how the macro **FNpush** could be written to cope with either a full or empty stack.

The variable **fullStack** is a global which is defined at the start of the program to **TRUE** if we are assembling for a full stack and **FALSE** if we want an empty one.

```
10000 DEF  FNpush(first,last)
10010 IF  fullStack  THEN
10020 [         OPT     pass
10030           STMFD   R13!,{first,last}
10040 ]
10050 ELSE
10060 [         OPT     pass
10070           STMED   R13!,{first,last}
10080 ]
10090 ENDIF
10100 =""
```

Most features of dedicated assemblers can be implemented using a combination of BBC BASIC and the BASIC assembler. For example, some assemblers have a **WHILE** loop directive which can be used to assemble repeated instructions which would be tedious (and maybe error prone) to type. The BASIC **WHILE** (or **FOR** or **REPEAT**) loops can be used to similar effect. The macro below implements a 'fill memory' function. It takes a count and a byte value, and stores the given number of bytes in the object code.

```
10000 DEF  FNfill(byte,count)
10010 IF  count=0  THEN  =""
10020 LOCAL  i
10030 FOR  i=1  TO  count
10040 [         OPT     pass
10050           EQUB    byte
10060 ]
10070 NEXT  i
10080 [         OPT     pass
10090           ALIGN
10100 ]
10110 =""
```

Although we could have quite easily 'poked' the bytes into the code without using **EQUB**, the method we use guarantees that the effect of **FNfill** shows up on the assembly listing. It is important to keep what is printed in the listing consistent with what is actually going on, otherwise it becomes difficult to debug programs from the listing.

4.7 Calling machine code

Many of the example programs in the next two chapters are accompanied by short test routines. These are called from BASIC after the code has been assembled. To help you understand these programs, we describe the **CALL** statement and the **USR** function in this section.

The format of the **CALL** statement is:

```
CALL  <address>,[<parameters>]
```

The **<address>** is the location of the machine code that you want to execute. The optional **<parameters>** are BASIC variables, separated by commas.

When the called routine starts to execute, it finds its registers set-up by BASIC. We won't describe the full extent of what BASIC provides for the machine code program, but instead point out the most useful features. First, R0 to R7 are set-up from the values of eight of the system integer variables (A% etc). So, R0 holds the contents of A%, R1 is initialised from B%, and so on, up to R7 which has been loaded from H%.

R9 points to the list of parameters, and R10 contains the number of parameters that followed the **<address>**. This may be zero, as the parameters are optional. The data to which R9 points is a list of pairs of words. There is one word-pair for each parameter.

The first word contains the address of the variable, i.e. where its value is stored in memory. The second word holds the type of the variable. From this, the meaning of the data addressed by the first word can be determined. The main types are as follows:

Type	**Meaning**
0	Single byte, e.g. **?addr**
4	Integer, e.g. **fred%**, **!fred**, **fred%(10)**
5	Real, e.g. **fred**, **|fred**, **fred(10)**
128	String, e.g. **fred$**, **fred$(10)**
129	String, e.g. **$fred**

The type-128 string value consists of five bytes. The first four are the address of the contents of the string (i.e. the characters), and the fifth byte is the string's length. A type-129 string is a sequence of bytes terminated by a carriage-return character, and the address word points to the first character of the string. Note that the data values can have any alignment, so to access them you must use a general-alignment routine of the type presented in Chapter Six.

It is important to realise that the word-pairs describing parameters are in reverse order. This means that the word pointed to by R9 is the address of the *last* parameter's value. The next word is the type of the last parameter, and the one after that is the address of the penultimate parameter, and so on. Obviously if there is only one parameter, this rerversal does not matter.

The final registers of importance are R13, which is BASIC's stack pointer, and R14, the link register. BASIC's (full, descending) stack may be used by the called routine, as long as the stack pointer ends up with the same value it had on entry to the routine. R14 contains the return address, as if the routine had been called with a **BL** instruction. This enables the routine to return to BASIC with an instruction such as:

```
MOV     pc,R14
```

The **USR** function is used in a similar way to **CALL**. There are two important differences. First, it cannot take parameters, so a typical use would be:

```
PRINT  ~USR  address
```

Second, it returns a result. This result is the contents of R0 on return from the machine code. There are several examples of **USR** in the next two chapters.

4.8 Summary

In this chapter we have looked at one of the assemblers available to the ARM programmer. Because it is part of ARM BASIC, it is straightforward to use. Although the assembler itself is not overflowing with features, the fact that assembler and BASIC can be freely combined has many advantages. It is relatively easy to implement many of the features of 'professional' assemblers, such as macros and conditional assembly.

Finally we looked briefly at the **CALL** and **USR** keywords in BASIC, in preparation for their use in later chapters.

5. Assembly programming principles

The previous chapters have covered the ARM instruction set, and using the ARM assembler. Now we are in a position to start programming properly. Since we are assuming you can program in BASIC, most of this chapter can be viewed as a conversion course. It illustrates with examples how the programming techniques that you use when writing in a high-level language translate into assembler.

5.1 Control structures

Some theory

A program is made up of instructions which implement the solution to a problem. Any such solution, or algorithm, may be expressed in terms of a few fundamental concepts. Two of the most important are program decomposition and flow of control.

The composition of a program relates to how it is split into smaller units which solve a particular part of the problem. When combined, these units, or sub-programs, form a solution to the problem as a whole. In high-level languages such as BASIC and Pascal, the procedure mechanism allows the practical decomposition of programs into smaller, more manageable units. Down at the assembly language level, subroutines perform the same function.

Flow of control in a program is the order in which the instructions are executed. The three important types of control structure that have been identified are: the sequence, iteration, and decision.

An instruction sequence is simply the act of executing instructions one after another in the order in which they appear in the program. On the ARM, this action is a consequence of the PC being incremented after each instruction, unless it is changed explicitly.

The second type of control flow is decision: the ability to execute a sequence of instructions only if a certain condition holds (e.g. **IF...THEN...**). Extensions of this are the ability to take two separate, mutually exclusive paths (**IF**...**THEN**...**ELSE**...), and a multi-way decision based on some value (**ON**...**PROC**...). All of these structures are available to the assembly language programmer, but he has to be more explicit about his intentions.

Iteration means looping. Executing the same set of instructions over and over again is one of the computer's fortes. High-level languages provide constructs such as **REPEAT**..**UNTIL** and **FOR**...**NEXT** to implement iteration. Again, in assembler you have to spell out the desired action a little more explicitly, using backward (perhaps conditional) branches.

Some practice

Having talked about program structures in a fairly abstract way, we now look at some concrete examples. Because we are assuming you have some knowledge of BASIC, or similar high-level language, the structures found therein will be used as a starting point. We will present faithful copies of **IF**...**THEN**...**ELSE**, **FOR**...**NEXT** etc. using ARM assembler. However, one of the advantages of using assembly language is its versatility; you shouldn't restrict yourself to slavishly mimicking the techniques you use in BASIC, if some other more appropriate method suggests itself.

Position-independence

Some of the examples below (for example the **ON**...**PROC** implementation using a branch table) may seem slightly more complex than necessary. In particular, addressing of data and routines is performed not by loading addresses into registers, but by performing a calculation (usually 'hidden' in an **ADR** directive) to obtain the same address. This seemingly needless complexity is due to a desire to make the programs position-independent.

Position-independent code has the property that it will execute correctly no matter where in memory it is loaded. In order to possess this property, the code must contain no references to absolute objects. That is, any internal data or routines accessed must be referenced with respect to some fixed point in the program. As the offset from the required location to the fixed point remains constant, the address of the object may be calculated regardless of where the program was loaded. Usually, addresses are calculated with respect to the current instruction. You would often see instructions of the form:

```
.here   ADD ptr,  pc,  #object-(here+8)
```

to obtain the address of **object** in the register **ptr**. The +8 part occurs because the PC is always two instructions (8 bytes) further on than the instruction which is executing, due to pipelining.

It is because of the frequency with which this calculation crops up that the **ADR** directive is provided. As we explained in Chapter Four, the line above could be written:

```
    ADR     ptr,  object
```

There is no need for a label: BASIC performs the calculation using the current value of P%.

Instead of using PC offsets, a program can also access its data using base-relative addressing. In this scheme, a register is chosen to store the base address of the program's data. It is initialised in some position-independent way at the start of the program, then all data accesses are relative to this. The ARM's register-offset address mode in **LDR** and **STR** make this quite a straightforward way of accessing data.

Why strive for position-independence? In a typical ARM system, the programs you write will be loaded into RAM, and may have to share that RAM with other programs. The operating system will find a suitable location for the program and load it there. As 'there' might be anywhere in the available memory range, your program can make no assumptions about the location of its internal routines and data. Thus all references must be relative to the PC. It is for this reason that branches use offsets instead of absolute addresses, and that the assembler provides the

```
    LDR     <dest>,<expression>
```

form of **LDR** and **STR** to automatically form PC-relative addresses.

Many microprocessors (especially the older, eight-bit ones) make it impossible to write position-independent code because of unsuitable instructions and architectures. The ARM makes it relatively easy, and you should take advantage of this.

Of course, there are bound to be some absolute references in the program. You may have to call external subroutines in the operating system. The usual way of doing this is to use a **SWI**, which implicitly calls absolute address &0000008. Pointers handed to the program by memory-allocation routines will be absolute, but as they are external to the program, this doesn't matter. The thing to avoid is absolute references to internal objects.

Sequences

These barely warrant a mention. As we have already implied, ARM instructions execute sequentially unless the processor is instructed to do otherwise. Sequence of high-level assignments:

```
LET a = b+c
LET d = b-c
```

would be implemented by a similar sequence of ARM instructions:

```
ADD     ra, rb, rc
SUB     rd, rb, rc
```

IF-type conditions

Consider the BASIC statement:

```
IF a=b THEN count=count+1
```

This maps quite well into the following ARM sequence:

```
CMP     ra, rb
ADDEQ   count, count, #1
```

In this and other examples, we will assume operands are in registers to avoid lots of **LDR**s and **STR**s. In practice, you may find a certain amount of processor-to-memory transfer has to be made.

The ARM's ability to execute any instruction conditionally enables us to make a straightforward conversion from BASIC. Similarly, a simple **IF**..**THEN**...**ELSE** such as this one

```
IF val<0 THEN sign=-1 ELSE sign=1
```

leads to the ARM equivalent:

```
TEQ     val, #0
MVNMI   sign, #0
MOVPL   sign, #1
```

The opposite conditions (**MI** and **PL**) on the two instructions make them mutually exclusive (i.e. one and only one of them will be executed after the **TEQ**), corresponding to the same property in the **THEN** and **ELSE** parts of the BASIC statement.

There is usually a practical limit to how many instructions may be executed conditionally in one sequence. For example, one of the conditional instructions may itself affect the flags, so the original condition no longer holds. A multi-word **ADD** will need to affect the carry flag, so this operation couldn't be performed using conditional execution. The solution (and the *only* method that most processors can use) is to conditionally branch over unwanted instructions.

Below is an example of a two-word add which executes only if R0=R1:

```
        CMP     R0, R1
        BNE     noAdd
        ADDS    lo1, lo1, lo2
        ADC     hi1, hi1, hi2
  .noAdd    ....
```

Notice that the condition used in the branch is the opposite to that under which the **ADD** is to be performed. Here is the general translation of the BASIC statements:

```
    IF cond THEN sequence1 ELSE sequence2  statement

    ;'ARM' version
    ;Obtain <cond>
    B<NOT cond>   seq2        ;If <cond> fails then jump to ELSE
    sequence1                 ;Otherwise do the THEN part
           ...
    BAL     endSeq2           ;Skip over the ELSE part
.seq2
    sequence2                 ;This gets executed if <cond> fails
           ...
.endSeq2
    statement                 ;The paths re-join here
```

At the end of the **THEN** sequence is an unconditional branch to skip the **ELSE** part. The two paths rejoin at **endSeq2**.

It is informative to consider the relative timings of skipped instructions and conditionally executed ones. Suppose the conditional sequence consists of X group one instructions. The table below gives the timings in cycles for the cases when they are executed and not executed, using each method:

	Branch	Conditional
Executed	s + Xs	Xs
Not executed	2n+s	Xs

In the case where the instructions are executed, the branch method has to execute the un-executed branch, giving an extra cycle. This gives us the rather predictable result that if the conditional sequence is only one instruction, the conditional execution method should always be used.

When the sequence is skipped because the condition is false, the branch method takes 2n+s, or the equivalent to 5s cycles. The conditional branch method takes one s cycles for each un-executed instruction. So, if there are four or fewer instructions, at least one cycle is saved using conditional instructions. Of course, whether this makes the program execute any faster depends on the ratio between failures and successes of the condition.

Before we leave the **IF**-type constructions, we present a nice way of implementing conditions such as:

```
IF a=1 OR a=5 OR a=12...
```

It uses conditional execution:

```
TEQ      a,#1
TEQNE    a,#5
TEQNE    a,#12
BNE      failed
```

If the first **TEQ** gives an **EQ** result (i.e. **a**=1), the next two instructions are skipped and the sequence ends with the desired flag state. If **a**<>1, the next **TEQ** is executed, and again if this gives an **EQ** result, the last instruction is skipped. If neither of those two succeed, the result of the whole sequence comes from the final **TEQ**.

Another useful property of **TEQ** is that it can be used to test the sign and zero-ness of a register in one instruction. So a three-way decision could be made according to whether an operand was less than zero, equal to zero, or greater than zero:

```
TEQ      R0,#0
BMI      neg
BEQ      zero
BPL      plus
```

In this example, one of three labels is jumped to according to the sign of R0. Note that the last instruction could be an unconditional branch, as **PL** must be true if we've got that far.

The sequence below performs the BASIC assignment **a=ABS(a)** using conditional instructions:

```
TEQ      a,  #0
RSBMI    a,  #0   ;if a<0 then a=0-a
```

As you have probably realised, conditional instructions allow the elegant expression of many simple types of **IF**... construct.

Multi-way branches

Often, a program needs to take one of several possible actions, depending on a value or a condition. There are two main ways of implementing such a branch, depending on the tests made.

If the action to be taken depends on one of a few specific conditions, it is best implemented using explicit comparisons and branches. For example, suppose we wanted to take one of three actions depending on whether the character in the lowest byte of R0 was a letter, a digit or some other character. Assuming that the character set being used is ASCII, then this can be achieved thus:

```
    CMP    R0,#ASC"0" ;Less than the lowest digit?
    BCC    doOther    ;Yes, so must be 'other'
    CMP    R0,#ASC"9" ;Is it a digit?
    BLS    doDigit    ;Yes
    CMP    R0,#ASC"A" ;Between digits and upper case?
    BCC    doOther    ;Yes, so 'other'
    CMP    R0,#ASC"Z" ;Is it upper case?
    BLS    doLetter   ;Yes
    CMP    R0,#ASC"a" ;Between upper and lower case?
    BLT    doOther    ;Yes, so 'other'
    CMP    R0,#ASC"z" ;Lower case?
    BHI    doOther    ;No, so 'other'
.doLetter
    ....
    B      nextChar   ;Process next character
.doDigit
    ....
    B      nextChar   ;Process next character
.doOther
    ....
.nextChar
    ....
```

Note that by the time the character has been sorted out, the flow of control has been divided into three possible routes. To make the program easier to follow, the three destination labels should be close to each other. It is very possible that after each routine has done its job, the three paths will converge again into a single thread. To make this clear, each routine is terminated by a commented branch to the meeting point.

A common requirement is to branch to a given routine according to a range of values. This is typified by BASIC's **ON...PROC** and **CASE** statements. For example:

```
ON x PROCadd,PROCdelete,PROCamend,PROClist ELSE PROCerror
```

According to whether **x** has the value 1, 2, 3 or 4, one of the four procedures listed is executed. The **ELSE**... part allows for **x** containing a value outside of the expected range.

One way of implementing an **ON**... type structure in assembly language is using repeated comparisons:

```
    CMP choice,  #1     ;Check against lower limit
    BCC error           ;Lower, so error
    BEQ add             ;choice = 1 so add
    CMP choice,  #3     ;Check for 2 or 3
    BLT delete          ;choice = 2 so delete
    BEQ amend           ;choice = 3 so amend
    CMP choice,  #4     ;Check against upper limit
    BEQ list            ;If choice = 4 list else error
.error
    .....
```

Although this technique is fine for small ranges, it becomes large and slow for wide ranges of **choice**. A better technique in this case it to use a branch table. A list of branches to the routines is stored near the program, and this is used to branch to the appropriate routine. Below is an implementation of the previous example using this technique.

```
DIM org 200
choice = 0
t = 1
sp = 13
link = 14

REM Range of legal values
min = 1
max = 4
WriteS = 1
NewLine = 3
FOR pass=0 TO 2 STEP 2
P%=org
[ opt pass
;Multiway branch in ARM assembler
;choice contains code, min..max of routine to call
;If out of range, error is called
;
   STMFD   (sp)!,{t,link}
   SUBS    choice, choice, #min ;Choice <min?
   BCC     error                ;Yes, so error
   CMP     choice, #max-min     ;Choice >max?
   BHI     error                ;Yes, so error
   ADR     link, return         ;Set-up return address
   ADR     t,table              ;Get address of table base
   ADD     PC, t, choice, LSL #2;Jump to table+choice*4
;
 .error
   SWI     WriteS
   EQUS    "Range error"
   EQUB    0
   ALIGN
;
 .return
   SWI     NewLine
   LDMFD   (sp)!,{t,PC}
;
```

```
;
;Table of branches to routines
.table
  B       add
  B       delete
  B       amend
  B       list
;
.add
  SWI     WriteS
  EQUS    "Add command"
  EQUB    0
  ALIGN
  MOV     PC,link
;
.delete
  SWI     WriteS
  EQUS        "Delete command"
  EQUB    0
  ALIGN
  MOV     PC,link
;
.amend
  SWI     WriteS
  EQUS    "Amend command"
  EQUB    0
  ALIGN
  MOV     PC,link
;
.list
  SWI     WriteS
  EQUS    "List command"
  EQUB    0
  ALIGN
  MOV     PC,link
]
NEXT
REPEAT
   INPUT "Choice ",A%
   CALLorg
UNTIL FALSE
```

The first four lines check the range of the value in **choice**, and call **error** if it is outside of the range **min** to **max**. It is important to do this, otherwise a branch might be made to an invalid entry in the branch table. The first test uses **SUBS** instead of **CMP**, so choice is adjusted to the range 0 to **max-min** instead of **min** to **max**.

Next, the return address is placed in R14. The routines **add**, **delete** etc. return as if they had been called using **BL**, i.e. use a return address in R14. To do this, we use **ADR** to place the address of the label **return** into R14, this being where we want to resume execution.

The next **ADR** obtains the base address of the jump table in the register **t**. Finally, the **ADD** multiplies **choice** by 4 (using two left shifts) and adds this offset to the table's base address. The result of the addition is placed in the program counter. This causes execution to jump to the branch instruction in the table that was denoted by **choice**. From there, the appropriate routine is called, with the return address still in R14.

As we mentioned in the position-independent code section, this may seem a little bit involved just to jump to one of four locations. Remember though that the technique will work for an arbitrary number of entries in the table, and will work at whatever address the program is loaded.

Loops

Looping is vital to any non-trivial program. Many problems have solutions that are expressed in an iterative fashion. There are two important classes of looping construct. The first is looping while, or until, a given condition is met (e.g. **REPEAT** and **WHILE** loops in BASIC). The second is looping for a given number of iterations (e.g. **FOR** loops). In fact, the second class is really a special case of the general conditional loop, the condition being that the loop has iterated the correct number of times.

An important characteristic of any looping construct is where the test of the looping condition is made. In BASIC **REPEAT** loops, for example, the test is made at the corresponding **UNTIL**. This means that the instructions in the loop are always executed at least once. Consider this example:

```
REPEAT
    IF a>b THEN a=a-b ELSE b=b-a
UNTIL a=b
```

This is a simple way to find the greatest common divisor (GCD) of **a** and **b**. If **a=b** (and **a**<>0) when the loop is entered, the result is an infinite loop as on the first iteration **b=b-a** will be executed, setting **b** to 0. From then on, **a=a-0** will be executed, which will never make **a=b**.

The **WHILE** loop tests the condition at the 'top', before its statements have been executed at all:

```
WHILE a<>b
    IF a>b THEN a=a-b ELSE b=b-a
ENDWHILE
```

This time, if **a=b**, the condition at the top will fail, so the loop will never be executed, leaving **a=b**=GCD(**a**,**b**).

Below are the two ARM equivalents of the **REPEAT** and **WHILE** loop versions of the GCD routine:

```
;Find the GCD of ra,rb.
;Fallible version using 'repeat' loop
.repeat
    CMP     ra,rb        ;REPEAT IF a>b
    SUBGT   ra,ra,rb     ;    THEN a=a-b
    SUBLE   rb,rb,ra     ;    ELSE b=b-a
    CMP     ra,rb        ;UNTIL
    BNE     repeat       ;a=b
;
;Find GCD of ra,rb, using 'while' loop
.while
    CMP     ra,rb        ;WHILE a<>b
    BNE     endwhile
    SUBGT   ra,ra,rb     ;    IF a>b THEN a=a-b
    SUBLE   rb,rb,ra     ;             ELSE b=b-a
    B       while        ;ENDWHILE
.endwhile
```

Notice that the difference between the two is that the **WHILE** requires a forward branch to skip the instructions in the body of the loop. This is not a problem for an assembler, which has to cope with forward references to be of any use at all. In an interpreted language like BASIC, though, the need to scan through a program looking for a matching **ENDWHILE** is something of a burden, which is why some BASIC's don't have such structures.

Because both of the code sequences above are direct translations of high-level versions, they are indicative of what we might expect a good compiler to produce. However, we are better than any compiler, and can optimise both sequences slightly by a bit of observation. In the first loop, we branch back to an instruction which we have just executed, wasting a little time. In the second case, we can use the conditional instructions to eliminate the first branch entirely. Here are the hand-coded versions:

```
;Fallible version using 'repeat'
    CMP     ra,rb        ;REPEAT IF a>b
.repeat
    SUBGT   ra,ra,rb     ;    THEN a=a-b
    SUBLE   rb,rb,ra     ;    ELSE b=b-a
    CMP     ra,rb        ;UNTIL
    BNE     repeat       ;a=b
;
;Find GCD of ra,rb, using 'while' loop
.while
    CMP     ra,rb        ;REPEAT
    SUBGT   ra,ra,rb     ;    IF a>b THEN a=a-b
    SUBLT   rb,rb,ra     ;         ELSE IF a<b b=b-a
    BNE     while        ;UNTIL a=b    endwhile
```

By optimising, we have converted the **WHILE** loop into a **REPEAT** loop with a slightly different body.

In general, a **REPEAT**-type structure is used when the processing in the 'body' of the loop will be needed at least once, whereas **WHILE**-type loops have to be used in situations where the 'null' case is a distinct possibility. For example, string handling routines in the BASIC interpreter have to deal with zero-length strings, which often means a **WHILE** looping structure is used. (See the string-handling examples later.)

A common special case of the **REPEAT** loop is the infinite loop, expressed as:

```
REPEAT
    REM do something
UNTIL FALSE
```

or in ARM assembler:

```
.loop
;   do something
    BAL loop
```

Programs which exhibit this behaviour are often interactive ones which take an arbitrary amount of input from the user. Again the BASIC interpreter is a good example. The exit from such programs is usually through some 'back door' method (e.g. calling another program) rather than some well-defined condition.

Since **FOR** loops are a special case of general loops, they can be expressed in terms of them. The **FOR** loop in BBC BASIC exhibits a **REPEAT**-like behaviour, in that the test for termination is performed at the end, and it executes at least once. Below is a typical **FOR** loop and its **REPEAT** equivalent:

```
REM A typical for loop
FOR ch=32 TO 126
    VDU ch
NEXT ch

REM REPEAT loop equivalent
ch=32
REPEAT
    VDU ch
    ch=ch+1
UNTIL ch>126
```

The initial assignment is placed just before the **REPEAT**. The body of the **REPEAT** is the same as that for the **FOR**, with the addition of the incrementing of **ch** just before the condition. The condition is that **ch** is greater than the limit given in the **FOR** statement.

We can code the **FOR** loop in ARM assembler by working from the **REPEAT** loop version:

```
;Print characters 32..126 using a FOR loop-type construct
;R0 holds the character
    MOV     R0, #32         ;Init the character
.loop
    SWI     WriteC      ;Print it
    ADD     R0, R0, #1 ;Increment it
    CMP     R0, #126    ;Check the limit
    BLE     loop        ;Loop if not finished
;
```

Very often, we want to do something a fixed number of times, which could be expressed as a loop beginning **FOR i=1 TO n**... in BASIC. When such loops are encountered in assembler, we can use the fact that zero results of group one instructions can be made to set the Z flag. In such cases, the updating of the looping variable and the test for termination can be combined into one instruction.

For example, to print ten stars on the screen:

```
FOR i=1 TO 10
    PRINT "*";
NEXT i
```

could be re-coded in the form:

```
;Print ten stars on the screen
;R0 holds the star character, R1 the count
    MOV     R0,#ASC"*" ;Init char to print
    MOV     R1,#10      ;Init count
.loop
    SWI     WriteC      ;Print a star
    SUBS    R1,R1,#1    ;Next
    BNE     loop
;
```

The **SUBS** will set the Z flag after the tenth time around the loop (i.e. when R1 reaches 0), so we do not have to make an explicit test.

Of course, if the looping variable's current value was used in the body of the loop, this method could not be used (unless the loop was of the form **FOR i=n TO 1 STEP -1**...) as we are counting down from the limit, instead of up from 1.

Some high-level languages provide means of repeating a loop before the end or exiting from the current loop prematurely. These two looping 'extras' are typified by the `continue` and `break` statements in the C language. `Continue` causes a jump to be made to just after the last statement inside the current `FOR`, `WHILE` or `REPEAT`-type loop, and `break` does a jump to the first statement after the current loop.

Because `continue` and `break` cause the flow of control to diverge from the expected action of a loop, they can make the program harder to follow and understand. They are usually only used to 'escape' from some infrequent or error condition. Both constructs may be implemented in ARM using conditional or unconditional branches.

5.2 Subroutines and procedures

We have now covered the main control flow structures. Programs written using just these constructs would be very large and hard to read. The sequence, decision and loop constructs help to produce an ordered solution to a given problem. However, they do not contribute to the division of the problem into smaller, more manageable units. This is where subroutines come in.

Even the most straightforward of problems that one is likely to use computer to solve can be decomposed into a set of simpler, shorter sub-programs. The motivations for performing this decomposition are several. Humans can only take in so much information at once. In terms of programming, a page of listing is a useful limit to how much a programmer can reasonably be expected to digest in one go. Also, by implementing the solution to a small part of a problem, you may be writing the same part of a later program. It is surprising how much may be accomplished using existing 'library' routines, without having to re-invent the wheel every time.

The topics of program decomposition and top-down, structured programming are worthy of books in their own right, and it is recommended that you consult these if you wish to write good programs in any language. The discipline of structured programming is even more important in assembler than in, say, Pascal, because it is easier to write treacherously unreadable code in assembler.

A minimal decomposition of most programs is shown in the block diagram overleaf. Data is taken in, processed in some way, then results output. If you think about it, most programs would be rather boring if they depended on absolutely no external stimulus for their results.

Once the input, processing and output stages have been identified, work can begin on solving these individual parts. Almost invariably this will involve further decomposition, until eventually a set of routines will be obtained which can be written directly in a suitably small number of basic instructions.

The way in which these routines are linked together, and how they communicate with each other, are the subjects of the next sections.

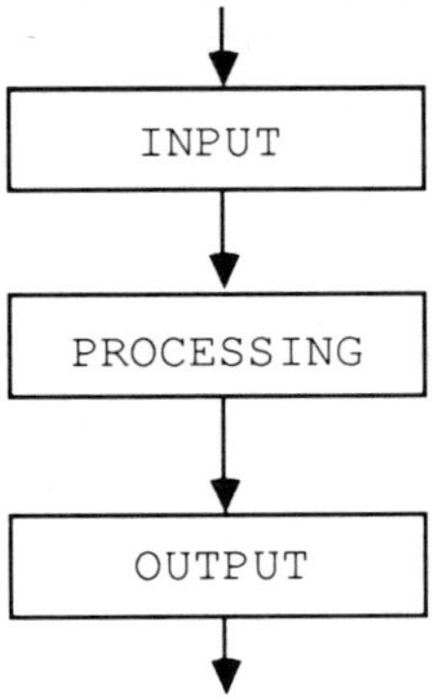

A minimal useful program

Branch and link

The ARM **BL** instruction is a subroutine-calling primitive. Primitive in this context means an operation which is implemented at the lowest level, with no more hidden detail.

Recall from Chapter Three that **BL** causes a branch to a given address, and stores the return address in R14. We will illustrate the use of **BL** to call the three routines which solve a very simple problem. This may be expressed as follows: repeatedly read a single character from the keyboard and if it is not the NUL character (ASCII code 0), print the number of 1 bits in the code.

For comparison, the BASIC program below solves the problem using exactly the same structure as the following ARM version:

```
REPEAT ch = FNreadChar
    IF  ch<>0  PROCoutput(FNprocess(ch))
UNTIL  ch=0
END
REM  ****************************************
DEF  FNreadChar=GET
REM  ****************************************
```

```
DEF FNprocess(ch)
    LOCAL  count
    count=0
    REPEAT
        count=count  +  ch  MOD  2
        ch=ch  DIV  2
    UNTIL  ch=0
=count
REM  *******************************************
DEF PROCoutput(num)
    PRINT  num
ENDPROC
```

There are four entities, separated by the lines of asterisks. At the top is the 'main program'. This is at the highest level and is autonomous: no other routine calls the program. The next three sections are the routines which the main program uses to solve the problem. As this is a fairly trivial example, none of the subroutines calls any other; they are all made from primitive instructions. Usually (and especially in assembly language where primitives are just that), these 'second level' routines would call even simpler ones, and so on.

Below is the listing of the ARM assembler version of the program:

```
DIM  org  200
sp  =  13
link  =  14
REM  SWI  numbers
WriteC  =  0
NewLine  =  3
ReadC  =  4
FOR  pass=0  TO  2  STEP  2
P%=org
[  opt  pass
;Read  characters  and  print  the  number  of  1  bits  in  the
;ASCII  code,  as  long  as  the  code  isn't  zero.
  STMFD   (sp)!,{link}   ;  Save  return  address
.repeat
  BL      readChar        ;Get  a  character  in  R0
  CMP     R0,#0           ;Is  it  zero?
  LDMEQFD (sp)!,{PC}      ;Yes,  so  return  to  caller
  BL      process         ;Get  the  count  in  R1
  BL      output          ;Print  R1  as  a  digit
  B       repeat          ;Do  it  again
;
;
;readChar  -  This  returns  a  character  in  R0
;All  other  registers  preserved
;
.readChar
  SWI     ReadC           ;Call  the  OS  for  the  read
  MOV     PC,  link       ;Return  using  R14
;
```

```
;process - This counts the number of 1s in R0 bits 0..7
;It returns the result in R1
;On exit, R1=count, R0=0, all others preserved
;
.process
  AND     R0, R0, #&FF  ;Zero bits 8..31 of R0
  MOV     R1, #0        ;Init the bit count
.procLoop
  MOVS    R0, R0, LSR #1;DIV 2 and get MOD 2 in carry
  ADC     R1, R1, #0    ;Add carry to count
  BNE     procLoop      ;More to do
  MOV     PC, link      ;Return with R1=count
;
;output - print R1 as a single digit
;On exit, R0=R1 + "0", all others preserved
;
.output
  ADD     R0, R1,#ASC"0";Convert R1 to ASCII in R0
  SWI     WriteC        ;Print the digit
  SWI     NewLine       ;And a newline
  MOV     PC, link      ;Return
]
NEXT
CALL org
```

Because of the way in which the program closely follows the BASIC version, you should not have much difficulty following it. Here are some points to note. In the BASIC version, two of the subroutines, **process** and **readChar**, are functions and **print** is a procedure. In the ARM version, there is no such obvious distinction in the way the routines are called. However, the fact that **process** and **readChar** return values to their caller makes them equivalent to function, whereas process, which returns no value of use to the caller, is a procedure equivalent.

At the start of each routine is a short description of what it does and how it affects the registers. Such documentation is the bare minimum that you should provide when writing a routine, so that problems such as registers being changed unexpectedly are easier to track down. In order to do this when the operating system routines are used (e.g. the **SWI WriteC** call), you have to know how those routines affect the registers. This information should be provided in the system documentation. For now, we assume that no registers are altered except those in which results are returned, e.g. R0 in **SWI ReadC**.

In the routine **process** we use the ability to (a) set the C flag from the result of shifting an **<rhs>** operand, and (b) preserve the state of the Z flag over the **ADC** by not specifying the **S** option. This enables us to write an efficient three-instruction version of the BASIC loop.

The routine **output** assumes that the codes of the digit symbols run contiguously from 0, 1, ...9. Using this assumption it is a simple matter to convert the binary number 1..8 (remember &00 will never have its 1 bits counted) into the equivalent printable code. As the ASCII code exhibits the desired contiguous property, and is almost universally used for character representation, the assumption is a safe one.

As none of the routines change the link register, R14, they all return using a simple move from the link register to the PC. We do not bother to use **MOVS** to restore the flags too, as they are not expected by the main program to be preserved.

If a subroutine calls another one using **BL**, then the link register will be overwritten with the return address for this later call. In order for the earlier routine to return, it must preserve R14 before calling the second routine. As subroutines very often call other routines (i.e. are 'nested'), to an arbitrary depth, some way is needed of saving any number of return addresses. The most common way of doing this is to save the addresses on the stack.

The program fragment below shows how the link register may be saved at the entry to a routine, and restored directly into the PC at the exit. Using this technique, any other registers which have to be preserved by the routine can be saved and restored in the same instructions:

```
;
 ;subEg.   This is an example of using the stack to save
;the return address of a subroutine.  In addition, R0,R1
;and R2 are preserved.
;
.subEg
    STMFD  (sp)!,{R0-R2,link};Save link and R0-R2
    ....                     ;Do some processing
    ....
    LDMFD  (sp)!,{R0-R2,pc}^ ;Load PC, flags and R0-R2
;
```

The standard forms of **LDM** and **STM** are used, meaning that the stack is a 'full, descending' one. Write-back is enabled on the stack pointer, since it almost always will be for stacking operations, and when the PC is loaded from the stack the flags are restored too, due to the **^** in the instruction.

Note that if the only 'routines' called are **SWI** ones, then there is no need to save the link register, R14, on the stack. Although **SWI** saves the PC and flags in R14, it is the supervisor mode's version of this register which is used, and the user's one remains intact.

Parameter passing

When values are passed to a routine, they are called the parameters, or arguments, of the routine. A routine performs some general task. When supplied with a particular set of arguments, it performs a more specific action (it has been parameterized, if you like), and the job it performs is usually the same for a particular set of arguments. When a routine returns one or more values to its caller, these values are known as the results of the routine.

The term 'subroutine' is usually applied to a primitive operation such as branch and link, which enables a section of code to be called then returned from. When a well-defined method of passing parameters is combined with the basic subroutine mechanism, we usually call this a procedure. For example, **`output`** in the example above is a procedure which takes a number between 0 and 9 in R1 and prints the digit corresponding to this. When a procedure is called in order to obtain the results it returns, it is called a function.

You may have heard the terms procedure and function in relation to high-level languages. The concept is equally valid in assembler, and when the procedures and functions of a high-level language are compiled (i.e. converted to machine code or assembler) they use just the primitive subroutine plus parameter passing mechanisms that we describe in this section.

In the example program of the previous section, the BASIC version used global variables as parameters and results, and the assembler version used registers. Usually, high-level languages provide a way of passing parameters more safely than using global variables. The use of globals is not desirable because (a) the caller and callee have to know the name of the variable being used and (b) global variables are prone to corruption by routines which do not 'realise' they are being used elsewhere in the program.

Using registers is just one of the ways in which arguments and results can be passed between caller and callee. Other methods include using fixed memory areas and the stack. Each method has its own advantages and drawbacks. These are described in the next few sections.

Register parameters

On a machine like the ARM, using the registers for the communication of arguments and results is the obvious choice. Registers are fairly plentiful (13 left after the PC, link and stack pointer have been reserved), and access to them is rapid. Remember that before the ARM can perform any data processing instructions, the operands must be loaded into registers. It makes sense then to ensure that they are already in place when the routine is called.

The operating system routines that we use in the examples use the registers for parameter passing. In general, registers which are not used to pass results back are preserved during the routine, i.e. their values are unaltered when control passes back to the caller. This is a policy you should consider using when writing your own routines. If the procedure itself preserves and restores the registers, there is no need for the caller to do so every time it uses the routine.

The main drawback of register parameters is that they can only conveniently be used to hold objects up to the size of a word - 32-bits or four bytes. This is fine when the data consists of single characters (such as the result of **SWI ReadC**) and integers. However, larger objects such as strings of characters or arrays of numbers cannot use registers directly.

Reference parameters

To overcome the problem of passing large objects, we resort to a slightly different form of parameter passing. Up until now, we have assumed that the contents of a register contain the value of the character or integer to be passed or returned. For example, when we use the routine called **process** in the earlier example, R0 held the value of the character to be processed, and on exit R1 contained the value of the count of the number one bits. Not surprisingly, this method is called call-by-value.

If instead of storing the object itself in a register, we store the object's address, the size limitations of using registers to pass values disappear. For example, suppose a routine requires the name of a file to process. It is obviously impractical to pass an arbitrarily long string using the registers, so we pass the address of where the string is stored in memory instead.

The example below shows how a routine called **wrchS** might be written and called. **WrchS** takes the address of a string in R1, and the length of the string in R2. It prints the string using **SWI WriteC**.

Note that the test program obtains the address in a position-independent way, using **ADR**. The first action of **wrchS** is to save R0 and the link register (containing the return address) onto the stack. The use of stacks for holding data was mentioned in ChapterThree, and we shall have more to say about them later. We save R0 because the specification in the comments states that all registers except R1 and R2 are preserved. Since we need to use R0 for calling **SWI WriteC**, its contents must be saved.

The main loop of the routine is of the **WHILE** variety, with the test at the top. This enables it to cope with lengths of less than or equal to zero. The **SUBS** has the dual effect of decreasing the length count by one and setting the flags for the termination condition. An **LDRB** is used to obtain the character from memory, and post-indexing is used to automatically update the address in R1.

```
DIM org 200
sp = 13
link = 14
cr = 13 : lf = 10
WriteC = 0
FOR pass=0 TO 2 STEP 2
P%=org
[ opt pass
;
;Example showing the use of wrchS
;
 .testWrchS
   STMFD   (sp)!,{link}        ;Save return address
   ADR     R1, string          ;Get address of string
   MOV     R2,#strEnd-string ;Load string length
   BL      wrchS               ;Print it
   LDMFD   (sp)!,{PC}          ;Return
;
 .string
   EQUS    "Test string"       ;The string to be printed
   EQUB    cr
   EQUB    lf
 .strEnd
;
;
;Subroutine to print a string addressed by R1
;R2 contains the number of bytes in the string
;On exit, R1 points the to byte after the string
;          R2 contains -1
;All other registers preserved
 .wrchS
   STMFD   (sp)!,  {R0,link} ;Save R0 and return address
 .wrchsLp
   SUBS    R2, R2, #1          ;End of string?
   LDMMIFD (sp)!,  {R0,PC}     ;Yes, so exit
   LDRB    R0, [R1], #1        ;Get a char and inc R1
   SWI     WriteC              ;Print this character
   B       wrchsLp             ;Next char
]
NEXT
CALL testWrchS
```

When the **LDMMI** is executed we restore R0 and return to the caller, using a single instruction. If we had not stored the link on the stack (as we did in the first instruction), an extra **MOV pc,link** would have been required to return.

Call-by-reference, or call-by-address is the term used when parameters are passed using their addresses instead of their values. When high-level languages use call-by-reference (e.g. **var** parameters in Pascal), there is usually a motive beyond the fact that registers cannot be used to store the value. Reference parameters are used to enable the called routine to alter the object whose address is passed. In effect, a reference parameter can be used to pass a result back, and the address of the result is passed to the routine in a register.

To illustrate the use of reference results, we present below a routine called **readS**. This is passed the address of an area of memory in R1. A string of characters is read from the keyboard using **SWI ReadC**, and stored at the given address. The length of the read string is returned in R0.

```
 DIM org 100, buffer 256
 WriteC = 0
 ReadC = 4
 NewLine = 3
 cr = &0D
 sp = 13
 link = 14
 FOR pass=0 TO 2 STEP 2
 P%=org
 [ opt pass
 ;
 ;readS. Reads a string from keyboard to memory
 ;addressed by R1. The string is terminated by the
character
 ;&0D (carriage return) On exit R0 contains the length of
 ;the string, including the CR
 ;All other registers are preserved
 ;
 .readS
    STMFD  (sp)!, {link}       ;Save return address
    MOV    R2, #0              ;Init the length
.readSlp
    SWI    ReadC               ;Get char in R0
    TEQ    R0, #cr             ;Was it carriage return?
    SWINE  WriteC              ;Echo the character if not
    STRB   R0, [R1, R2]        ;Store the char
    ADD    R2, R2, #1          ;Increment the count
    BNE    readSlp             ;If not CR, loop
    SWI    NewLine             ;Echo the newline
    MOV    R0, R2              ;Return count in R0 for USR
    LDMFD  (sp)!, {PC}         ;Return
 ]
 NEXT
 B%=buffer
```

```
PRINT"String:  ";
len%=USR  readS
PRINT"Length  was  ";len%
PRINT"String  was  "$buffer
```

This time, a **REPEAT**-type loop is used because the string will always contain at least one character, the carriage return. Of course, a routine such as this would not be very practical to use: there is no checking for a maximum string length; no action on special keys such as **DELETE** or **ESCAPE** is taken. It does, however, show how a reference parameter might be used to pass the address of a variable which is to be updated by the routine.

Parameter blocks

A parameter block, or control block, is closely related to reference parameters. When we pass a parameter block to a routine, we give it the address of an area of memory in which it may find one or more parameters. For example, suppose we wrote a routine to save an area of memory as a named file on the disk drive. Several parameters would be required:

Name of the file on the disk
Start address of data
End address (or length) of data
Load address of data
Execution address (in case it is a program)
Attributes (read, write etc.)

Now, all of these items may be passed in registers. If we assume the name is passed by address and has some delimiting character on the end, six registers would be required. Alternatively, the information could be passed in a parameter block, the start address of which is passed in a single register. The file save routine could access the component parts of the block using, for example

```
LDR    [base,#offset]
```

where **base** is the register used to pass the start address, and **offset** is the address of the desired word relative to **base**.

As the address of the parameter block is passed to the routine,the parameters may be altered as well as read. Thus parameter blocks are effectively reference parameters which may be used to return information in addition to passing it. For example, the parameter block set up for a disk load operation could have its entries updated from the data stored for the file in the disk catalog (load address, length etc.)

Parameter blocks are perhaps less useful on machines with generous register sets like the ARM than on processors which are less well-endowed, e.g. 8-bit micros such as the 6502. However, you should remember the advantage of only one register being needed to pass several parameters, and be ready to use the technique if appropriate.

Stack parameters

The final parameter passing technique which we will describe uses the stack to store arguments and results. In chapter three we described the **LDM** and **STM** instructions, for which the main use is dealing with a stack-type structure. Information is pushed on to a stack using **STM** and pulled from it using **LDM**. We have already seen how these instructions are used to preserve the return address and other registers.

To pass parameters on the stack, the caller must push them just before calling the routine. It must also make room for any results which it expects to be returned on the stack. The example below calls a routine which expects to find two arguments on the stack, and returns a single result. All items are assumed to occupy a single word.

```
;
;StackEg.   This shows how the stack might be used
;to pass arguments and receive results from a stack.
;Before entry, two arguments are pushed, and on exit a
;single result replaces them.   ;
.stackEg
    STMFD   (sp)!,{R0,R1} ;Save the arguments
    BL      stackSub      ;Call the routine
    LDMFD   (sp)!,{R0}    ;Get the result
    ADD     sp,sp,#8      ;'Lose' the arguments
    ....
    ....
.stackSub
    LDMFD   (sp)!,{R4,R5} ;Get the arguments
    ....                  ;Do some processing
    ....
    STMFD   (sp)!,{R2}    ;Save the result
    MOV     pc,link       ;Return
```

Looking at this code, you may think to yourself 'what a waste of time.' As soon as one routine pushes a value, the other pulls it again. It would seem much more sensible to simply pass the values in registers in the first place. Notice, though, that when **stackSub** is called, the registers used to set-up the stack are different from those which are loaded inside the routine. This is one of the advantages of stacked parameters: all the caller and callee need to know is the size, number and order of the parameters, not (explicitly) where they are stored.

In practice, it is rare to find the stack being used for parameter passing by pure assembly language programs, as it is straightforward to allocate particular registers. Where the stack scheme finds more use is in compiled high-level language procedures. Some languages, such as C, allow the programmer to assume that the arguments to a procedure can be accessed in contiguous memory locations. Moreover, many high-level languages allow recursive procedures, i.e. procedures which call themselves. Since a copy of the parameters is required for each invocation of a procedure, the stack is an obvious place to store them. See the Acorn ARM Calling Standard for an explanation of how high-level languages use the stack.

Although the stack is not often used to pass parameters in assembly language programs, subroutines frequently save registers in order to preserve their values across calls to the routine. We have already seen how the link register (and possibly others) may be saved using **STM** at the start of a procedure, and restored by **LDM** at the exit. To further illustrate this technique, the program below shows how a recursive procedure might use the stack to store parameters across invocations.

The technique illustrated is very similar to the way parameters (and local variables) work in BBC BASIC. All variables are actually global. When a procedure with the first line

```
DEF  PROCeg(int%)
```

is called using the statement **PROCeg(42)**, the following happens. The value of **int%** is saved on the stack. Then **int%** is assigned the value 42, and this is the value it has throughout the procedure. When the procedure returns using **ENDPROC**, the previous value of **int%** is pulled from the stack, restoring its old value.

The assembly language equivalent of this method is to pass parameters in registers. Just before a subroutine is called, registers which have to be preserved across the call are pushed, and then the parameter registers are set-up. When the routine exits, the saved registers are pulled from the stack.

There are several routines which are commonly used to illustrate recursion. The one used here is suitable because of its simplicity; the problem to be solved does not get in the way of showing how recursion is used. The Fibonacci sequence is a series of numbers thus:

0, 1, 1, 2, 3, 5, 8, 13, 21, 34, ...

where each number is the sum of its two predecessors. It can be expressed mathematically in terms of some functions:

f(0) = 0
f(1) = 1
f(n) = f(n-2) + f(n-1)

where f(n) means the nth number in the sequence starting from zero. It can easily be translated into a BASIC function:

```
DEF FNfib(n) IF n<=1 THEN =n ELSE =FNfib(n-2)+FNfib(n-1)
```

To convert this into ARM assembler, we will assume that the number **n** is passed in R1 and the result fib(**n**) returned in R0.

```
DIM org 200
link=14
sp=13
FOR pass=0 TO 2 STEP 2
P%=org

[ opt pass
;Fibonacci routine to return fib(n)
;On entry, R1 contains n
;On exit, R0 contains fib(n), R1 preserved, R2 corrupt
;
.fib
   CMP     R1,#1             ;See if it's an easy case
   MOVLE   R0,R1             ;Yes, so return it in R0
   MOVLE   PC,link           ;And return
   STMFD   (sp)!,{link}      ;Save return address
   SUB     R1,R1,#2          ;Get fib(n-2) in R0
   BL      fib
   STMFD   (sp)!,{R0}        ;Save it on the stack
   ADD     R1,R1,#1          ;Get fib(n-1) in R0
   BL      fib
   LDMFD   (sp)!,{R2}        ;Pull fib(n-2)
   ADD     R0,R0,R2          ;Add fib(n-2) and fib(n-1) in R0
   ADD     R1,R1,#1          ;Restore R1 to entry value
   LDMFD   (sp)!,{PC}        ;Return
]
NEXT
FOR B%=0 TO 25

    PRINT "Fib(";B%") is ";USR fib
NEXT B%
```

The routine does not use the stack in exactly the same way as BBC BASIC, but the saving of intermediate results on the stack enables `fib` to be called recursively in the same way. Note that it is important that on return R1 is preserved, i.e. contains **n**, as specified in the comments. This is because whenever `fib` is called recursively the caller expects R1 to be left intact so that it can calculate the next value correctly. In the cases when R1=0 or 1 on entry it is clearly preserved; in the other cases, by observation R1 is changed by -2, +1 and +1, i.e. there is no net change in its value.

You should note that, like a lot of routines that are expressed elegantly using recursion, this Fibonacci program becomes very inefficient of time and stack space for quite small values of **n**. This is due to the number of recursive calls made. (For an exercise you could draw a 'tree' of the calls for some start value, say 6.) A better solution is a counting loop. This is expressed in BASIC and ARM assembler below.

```
DEF  FNfib(n)
    IF n <= 1 THEN =n
    LOCAL f1,f2
    f2=0 : f1 = 1
    FOR i=0 TO n-2
        f1 = f1+f2
        f2 = f1-f2
    NEXT i
= f1

 DIM org 200
 i = 2          : REM Work registers
 f1 = 3
 f2 = 4
 sp = 13

 link = 14
 FOR pass=0 TO 2 STEP 2
 P%=org
 [ opt pass

 ;fib - using iteration instead of recursion
 ;On entry, R1 = n
 ;On exit, R0 = fib(n)
 ;
.fib
    CMP     R1,#1               ;Trivial test first
    MOVLE   R0,R1
    MOVLE   PC,link
    STMFD   (sp)!,{i,f1,f2,link} ;Save work registers and
link
    MOV     f1,#1               ;Initialise fib(n-1)
    MOV     f2,#0               ;and fib(n-2)
    SUB     i,R1,#2             ;Set-up loop count
.fibLp
    ADD     f1,f1,f2            ;Do calculation
    SUB     f2,f1,f2
    SUBS    i,i,#1
    BPL     fibLp               ;Until i reaches -1
    MOV     R0,f1               ;Return result in R0
    LDMFD   (sp)!,{i,f1,f2,PC};Restore and return
 ]
```

```
NEXT pass
FOR B%=0 TO 25

   PRINT"Fib(";B%;") is ";USR fib
NEXT B%
```

Summary

The main thrust of this chapter has been to show how some of the familiar concepts of high-level languages can be applied to assembler. Most control structures are easily implemented in terms of branches, though more complex ones (such as multi-way branching) can require slightly more work. This is especially true if the code is to exhibit the desirable property of position-indepence.

We also saw how parameters may be passed between routines - in registers, on the stack, or in parameter blocks. Using the stack has the advantage of allowing recursion, but is less efficient than passing information in registers.

6. Data structures

We have already encountered some of the ways in which data is passed between parts of a program: the argument and result passing techniques of the previous chapter.

In this chapter we concentrate more on the ways in which global data structures are stored, and give example routines showing typical data manipulation techniques.

Data may be classed as internal or external. For our purposes, we will regard internal data as values stored in registers or 'within' the program itself. External data is stored in memory allocated explicitly by a call to an operating system memory management routine, or on the stack.

6.1 Writing for ROM

A program's use of internal memory data may have to be restricted to read-only values. If you are writing a program which might one day be stored in a ROM, rather than being loaded into RAM, you must bear in mind that performing an instruction such as:

```
    STR     R0, label
```

will not have the desired effect if the program is executing in ROM. So, you must limit internal references to look-up tables etc. if you wish your code to be ROMmable. For example, the BBC BASIC interpreter only accesses locations internal to the program when performing tasks such as reading the tables of keywords or help information.

A related restriction on ROM code is that it should not contain any self-modifying instructions. Self-modifying code is sometimes used to alter an instruction just before it is executed, for example to perform some complex branch operation. Such techniques are regarded as bad practice, and something to be avoided, even in RAM programs. Obviously if you are tempted to write self-modifying code, you will have to cope with some pretty obscure bugs if the program is ever ROMmed.

Finally, the need for position-independence is an important consideration when you write code for ROM. A ROM chip may be fitted at any address in the ROM address space of the machine, and should still be expected to work.

The only time it is safe to write to the program area is in programs which will always, always, be RAM-based, e.g. small utilities to be loaded from disc. In fact, even RAM-based programs aren't entirely immune from this problem. The MEMC memory controller chip which is used in many ARM systems has the ability to make an area of memory 'read-only'. This is to protect the program from over-writing itself, or other programs in a multi-tasking system. Attempting to write to such a region will lead to an *abort*, as described in Chapter Seven.

It is a good idea, then, to only use RAM which has been allocated explicitly as workspace by the operating system, and treat the program area as 'read-only'.

6.2 Types of data

The interpretation of a sequence of bits in memory is entirely up to the programmer. The only assumption the processor makes is that when it loads a word from the memory addressed by the program counter, the word is a valid ARM instruction.

In this section we discuss the common types of data used in programs, and how they might be stored.

6.3 Characters

This is probably the most common data type, as communication between programs and people is usually character oriented. A character is a small integer whose value is used to stand for a particular symbol. Some characters are used to represent control information instead of symbols, and are called control codes.

By far the most common character representation is ASCII - American Standard Code for Information Interchange. We will only be concerned with ASCII in this book.

Standard ASCII codes are seven bits - representing 128 different values. Those in the range 32..126 stand for printable symbols: the letters, digits, punctuation symbols etc. An example is 65 (&41), which stands for the upper-case letter A. The rest 0..31 and 127 are control codes. These codes don't represent physical characters, but are used to control output devices. For example, the code 13 (&0D) is called carriage return, and causes an output device to move to the start of the current line.

Now, the standard width for a byte is eight bits, so when a byte is used to store an ASCII character, there is one spare bit. Previously (i.e. in the days of punched tape) this has been used to store a parity bit of the character.

This is used to make the number of 1 bits in the code an even (or odd) number. This is called even (or odd) parity. For example, the binary of the code for the letter A is 1000001. This has an even number of one bits, so the parity bit would be 0. Thus the code including parity for A is 01000001. On the other hand, the code for C is 1000011, which has an odd number of 1s. To make this even, we would store C with parity as 11000011. Parity gives a simple form of checking that characters have been sent without error over transmission lines.

As output devices have become more sophisticated and able to display more than the limited 95 characters of pure ASCII, the eighth bit of character codes has changed in use. Instead of this bit storing parity, it usually denotes another 128 characters, the codes for which lie in the range 128..255. Such codes are often called 'top-bit-set' characters, and represent symbols such as foreign letters, the Greek alphabet, symbol 'box-drawing' characters and mathematical symbols.

There is a standard (laid down by ISO, the International Standards Organisation) for top-bit-set codes in the range 160..255. In fact there are several sets of characters, designed for different uses. It is expected that many new machines, including ARM-based ones will adopt this standard.

The use of the top bit of a byte to denote a second set of character codes does not preclude the use of parity. Characters are simply sent over transmission lines as eight bits plus parity, but only stored in memory as eight bits.

When stored in memory, characters are usually packed four to each ARM word. The first character is held in the least significant byte of the word, the second in the next byte, and so on. This scheme makes for efficient processing of individual characters using the **LDRB** and **STRB** instructions.

In registers, characters are usually stored in the least significant byte, the other three bytes being set to zero. This is clearly wise as **LDRB** zeroes bits 8..31 of its destination register, and **STRB** uses bits 0..7 of the source register as its data.

Common operations on registers are translation and type testing. We cover translation below using strings of characters. Type testing involves discovering if a character is a member of a given set. For example, you might want to ascertain if a character is a letter. In programs which perform a lot of character manipulation, it is common to find a set of functions which return the type of the character in a standard register, e.g. R0.

These type-testing functions, or predicates, are usually given names like **isLower** (case) or **isDigit**, and return a flag indicating whether the character is a member of that type. We will adopt the convention that the character is in R0 on entry, and on exit all registers are preserved, and the carry flag is cleared if the character is in the named set, or set if it isn't. Below are a couple of examples: **isLower** and **isDigit**:

```
DIM org 100
sp = 1
link =14
WriteI = &100
NewLine = 3
Cflag = &20000000 : REM Mask for carry flag
FOR pass=0 TO 2 STEP 2
P%=org
[ opt pass
;
;Character type-testing predicates.
;On entry, R0 contains the character to be tested
;On exit C=0 if character in the set, C=1 otherwise
;All registers preserved
;
.isLower
    CMP     R0, #ASC"a"          ;Check lower limit
    BLT     predFail             ;Less than so return failure
    CMP     R0, #ASC"z"+1        ;Check upper limit
    MOV     pc, link             ;Return with appropriate Carry
.predFail
    TEQP    pc, #Cflag           ;Set the carry flag
    MOV     pc, link             ;and return
;
.isDigit
    CMP     R0, #ASC"0"          ;Check lower limit
    BLT     predFail             ;Lower so fail
    CMP     R0, #ASC"9"+1        ;Check upper limit
    MOV     pc, link             ;Return with appropriate Carry
;
;Test for isLower and isDigit
;If R0 is digit, 0 printed; if lower case, a printed
 ;
.testPred
    STMFD   (sp)!,{link}
    BL      isDigit
    SWICC   WriteI+ASC"0"
    BL      isLower
    SWICC   WriteI+ASC"a"
    SWI     NewLine
    LDMFD   (sp)!,{pc}
;
]
NEXT pass
```

```
REPEAT
    INPUT"Character  ",c$
    A%=ASCc$
    CALL  testPred
UNTIL  FALSE
```

The program uses two different methods to set the carry flag to the required state. The first is to use **TEQP**. Recall from Chapter Three that this can be used to directly set bits of the status register from the right hand operand. The variable **Cflag** is set to &20000000, which is bit mask for the carry flag in the status register. Thus the instruction

```
    TEQP    pc,  #Cflag
```

will set the carry flag and reset the rest of the result flags. The second method uses the fact that the **CMP** instruction sets the carry flag when the **<lhs>** is greater than or equal to its **<rhs>**. So, when testing for lower case letters, the comparison

```
    CMP     R0,#ASC"z"+1
```

will set the carry flag if R0 is greater than or equal to the ASCII code of z plus 1. That is, if R0 is greater than the code for z, the carry will be set, and if it is less than or equal to it (and is therefore a lower case letter), the carry will be clear. This is exactly the way we want it to be set-up to indicate whether R0 contains a lower case letter or not.

Strings of characters

When a set of characters is stored contiguously in memory, the sequence is usually called a string. There are various representations for strings, differentiated by how they indicate the number of characters used. A common technique is to terminate the string by a pre-defined character. BBC BASIC uses the carriage return character &0D to mark the end of its **$** indirection operator strings. For example, the string "**ARMENIA**" would be stored as the bytes

A	&41
R	&52
M	&4D
E	&45
N	&4E
I	&49
A	&41
cr	&0D

An obvious restriction of this type of string is that it can't contain the delimiter character.

The other common technique is to store the length of the string immediately before the characters - the language BCPL adopts this technique. The length may occupy one or more bytes, depending on how long a string has to be represented. By limiting it to a single byte (lengths between 0 and 255 characters) you can retain the byte-aligned property of characters. If, say, a whole word is used to store the length, then the whole string must be word aligned if the length is to be accessed conveniently. Below is an example of how the string "**ARMAMENT**" would be stored using a one-byte length:

```
len &08
A   &41
R   &52
M   &4D
A   &41
M   &4D
E   &45
N   &4E
T   &54
```

Clearly strings stored with their lengths may contain any character.

Common operations on strings are: copying a string from one place to another, counting the length of a string, performing a translation on the characters of a string, finding a sub-string of a string, comparing two strings, concatenating two strings. We shall cover some of these in this section. Two other common operations are converting from the binary to ASCII representation of a number, and vice versa. These are described in the next section.

Character translation

Translation involves changing some or all of the characters in a string. A common translation is the conversion of lower case letters to upper case, or vice versa. This is used, for example, to force filenames into upper case. Another form of translation is converting between different character codes, e.g. ASCII and the less popular EBCDIC.

Overleaf is a routine which converts the string at **strPtr** into upper case. The string is assumed to be terminated by CR.

```
DIM org 100, buff 100
cr = &0D
strPtr = 0
sp = 13
link = 14
carryBit = &20000000
FOR pass=0 TO 2 STEP 2
P%=org
[ opt pass
;toUpper. Converts the letters in the string at strPtr
;to upper case. All other characters are unchanged.
;All registers preserved
;R1 used as temporary for characters
;
toUpper
    STMFD   (sp)!,{R1,strPtr,link};Preserve  registers
.toUpLp
    LDRB    R1, [strPtr], #1        ;Get byte and inc ptr
    CMP     R1, #cr                 ;End of string?
    LDMEQFD (sp)!,{R1,strPtr,pc}    ;Yes, so return
    BL      isLower                 ;Check lower case
    BCS     toUpLp                  ;Isn't, so loop
    SUB     R1,R1,#ASC"a"-ASC"A"    ;Convert the case
    STRB    R1,[strPtr,#-1]         ;Save char back
    B       toUpLp                  ;Next char
;
.isLower
    CMP     R1,  #ASC"a"
    BLT     notLower
    CMP     R1,  #ASC"z"+1
    MOV     pc,link
.notLower
    TEQP    pc,#carryBit
    MOV     pc,link
]
NEXT
REPEAT
    INPUT"String  ",$buff
    A%=buff
    CALL toUpper
    PRINT"Becomes  "$buff
UNTIL FALSE
```

The program uses the fact that the upper and lower case letters have a constant difference in their codes under the ASCII character set. In particular, each lower case letter has a code which is 32 higher than its upper case equivalent. This means that once it has been determined that a character is indeed a letter, it can be changed to the other case by adding or subtracting 32. You can also swap the case by using this operation:

```
    EOR     R0, R0, #ASC"a"-ASC"A"      ;Swap case
```

The **EOR** instruction inverts the bit in the ASCII code which determines the case of the letter.

Comparing strings

The example routine in this section compares two strings. String comparison works as follows. If the strings are the same in length and in every character, they are equal. If they are the same up to the end of the shorter string, then that is the lesser string. If they are the same until a certain character, the relationship between the strings is the same as that between the corresponding characters at that position.

strCmp below compares the two byte-count strings at **str1** and **str2**, and returns with the flags set according to the relationship between them. That is, the zero flag is set if they are equal, and the carry flag is set if **str1** is greater than or equal to **str2**.

```
DIM org 200, buff1 100, buff2 100
REM str1 to char2 should be contiguous registers
str1 = 0
str2 = 1
len1 = 2
len2 = 3
index = 4
flags = len2
char1 = 5
char2 = 6
sp = 13
link = 14
FOR pass=0 TO 2 STEP 2
P%=org
[ opt pass
;strCmp. Compare the strings at str1 and str2. On exit,
;all registers preserved, flags set to the reflect the
;relationship between the strings.
;Registers used:
;len1, len2 - the string lengths. len1 is the shorter one
;flags - a copy of the flags from the length comparison
;index - the current character in the string
;char1, char2 - characters from each string
;NB len2 and flags can be the same register
;
.strCmp
;Save all registers
    STMFD  (sp)!,  {str1-char2,link}
    LDRB   len1,  [str1],  #1       ;Get the two lengths
    LDRB   len2,  [str2],  #1       ;and move pointers on
    CMP    len1,  len2              ;Find the shorter
    MOVGT  len1,  len2              ;Get shorter in len1
    MOV    flags,  pc               ;Save result
    MOV    index,  #0               ;Init index
.strCmpLp
```

```
        CMP     index, len1             ;End of shorter string?
        BEQ     strCmpEnd               ;Yes so result on lengths
        LDRB    char1, [str1, index]    ;Get a character from each
        LDRB    char2, [str2, index]
        ADD     index, index, #1        ;Next index
        CMP     char1, char2            ;Compare the chars
        BEQ     strCmpLp                ;If equal, next char
;
;Return with result of last character compare
;Store flags so BASIC can read them
;
        STR     pc,theFlags
        LDMFD   (sp)!,{str1-char2,pc}
;
;Shorter string exhausted so return with result of
;the comparison between the lengths
;
.strCmpEnd
        TEQP    flags, #0               ;Get flags from register
;
;Store flags so BASIC can read them
;
        STR     pc,theFlags
        LDMFD   (sp)!, {str1-char2,pc}
;
.theFlags
        EQUD    0
]
NEXT pass
carryBit = &20000000
zeroBit = &40000000
REPEAT
    INPUT'"String 1 ",s1$,"String 2 ",s2$
    ?buff1=LENs1$ : ?buff2=LENs2$
    $(buff1+1)=s1$
    $(buff2+1)=s2$
    A%=buff1
    B%=buff2
    CALL strCmp
    res = !theFlags
    PRINT "String 1 "
    IF res AND carryBit THEN PRINT">= "; ELSE PRINT "< ";
    PRINT "String 2"
    PRINT "String 1 ";
    IF res AND zeroBit THEN PRINT"= "; ELSE PRINT"<> ";
    PRINT "String 2"
UNTIL FALSE
```

Finding a sub-string

In text-handling applications, we sometimes need to find the occurrence of one string in another. The BASIC function **INSTR** encapsulates this idea.

The call

```
INSTR("STRING WITH PATTERN","PATTERN")
```

will return the integer 13, as the sub-string "**PATTERN**" occurs at character 13 of the first argument.

The routine listed below performs a function analogous to **INSTR**. It takes two arguments - byte-count string pointers - and returns the position at which the second string occurs in the first one. The first character of the string is character 1 (as in BASIC). If the sub-string does not appear in the main string, 0 is returned.

For a change, we use the stack to pass the parameters and return the result. It is up to the caller to reserve space for the result under the arguments, and to 'tidy up' the stack on return.

```
DIM org 400,mainString 40, subString 40
str1 = 0
str2 = 1
result = 2
len1 = 3
len2 = 4
char1 = 5
char2 = 6
index = 7
work = 8
sp = 13
link = 14
FOR pass=0 TO 2 STEP 2
P%=org
[ opt pass
;
;instr. Finds the occurence of str2 in str1. Arguments on
;the stack. On entry and exit, the stack contains:
;
;       result       word 2
;       str1         word 1
;       str2          <-- sp  word 0  plus 10 pushed words
;
;str1 is the main string, str2 the substring
;All registers are preserved. Result is 0 for no match
;
.instr
;Save work registers
    STMFD   (sp)!,{str1-work,link}
    LDR     str1,  [sp, #(work-str1+2+0)*4]  ;Get str1 pointer
    LDR     str2,  [sp, #(work-str1+2+1)*4]  ;and str2 pointer
    MOV     work,  str1          ;Save for offset calculation
    LDRB    len1,  [str1], #1  ;Get lengths and inc pointers
    LDRB    len2,  [str2], #1
.inLp1
```

```
    CMP     len1, len2          ;Quick test for failure
    BLT     inFail              ;Substr longer than main string
    MOV     index, #0           ;Index into strings
.inLp2
    CMP     index, len2         ;End of substring?
    BEQ     inSucc              ;Yes, so return with str2
    CMP     index, len1
    BEQ     inNext              ;End of main string so next try
    LDRB    char1, [str1, index] ;Compare characters
    LDRB    char2, [str2, index]
    ADD     index, index, #1     ;Inc index
    CMP     char1, char2         ;Are they equal?
    BEQ     inLp2               ;Yes, so next char
.inNext
    ADD     str1, str1, #1      ;Move onto next start in str2
    SUB     len1, len1, #1      ;It's one shorter now
    B       inLp1
.inFail
    MOV     work, str1          ;Make SUB below give 0
.inSucc
    SUB     str1, str1, work     ;Calc. pos. of sub string
    STR     str1,[sp,#(work-str1+2+2)*4] ;Save it in result
;Restore everything and return
    LDMFD   (sp)!,{str1-work,pc}
;
;Example of calling instr.
;Note that in order that the STM pushes the
;registers in the order expected by instr, the following
;relationship must exist. str2 < str1 < result
;
.testInstr
    ADR     str1,mainString      ;Address of main string
    ADR     str2,subString      ;Address of substring
    STMFD   (sp)!, {str1,str2,result,link} ;Push strings and
    BL      instr             ;room for the result. Call instr.
    LDMFD   (sp)!, {str1,str2,result} ;Load strings & result
    MOV     R0,result           ;Result in r0 for USR function
    LDMFD   (sp)!,{pc}
;
]
NEXT
    REPEAT
        INPUT"Main string 1 ",s1$ , "Substring 2 ",s2$
        ?mainString = LEN s1$
        ?subString = LEN s2$
        $(mainString+1) = s1$
        $(subString+1) = s2$
        pos = USR testInstr
        PRINT "INSTR("""s1$""","""s2$""") =";pos;
        PRINT " (";INSTR(s1$,s2$)")"
    UNTIL FALSE
```

The Note in the comments is to act as a reminder of the way in which multiple registers are stored. **STM** always saves lower numbered registers in memory before higher numbered ones. Thus if the correct ordering on the stack is to be obtained, register **str2** must be lower than **str1**, which must be lower than **result**. Of course, if this weren't true, correct ordering on the stack could still be achieved by pushing and pulling the registers one at a time.

6.4 Integers

The storage and manipulation of numbers comes high on the list of things that computers are good at. For most purposes, integer (as opposed to floating point or 'real') numbers suffice, and we shall discuss their representation and operations on them in this section.

Integers come in varying widths. As the ARM is a 32-bit machine, and the group one instructions operate on 32-bit operands, the most convenient size is obviously 32-bits. When interpreted as signed quantities, 32-bit integers represent a range of -2,147,483,648 to +2,147,483,647. Unsigned integers give a corresponding range of 0 to 4,294,967,295.

When stored in memory, integers are usually placed on word boundaries. This enables them to be loaded and stored in a single operation. Non word-aligned integer require two **LDR**s or **STR**s to move them in and out of the processor, in addition to some masking operations to 'join up the bits'.

It is somewhat wasteful of memory to use four bytes to store quantities which need only one or two bytes. We have already seen that characters use single bytes to hold an eight-bit ASCII code, and string lengths of up to 255 characters may be stored in a single byte. An example of two-byte quantities is BASIC line numbers (which may be in the range 0..65279 and so require 16 bits).

LDRB and **STRB** enable unsigned bytes to to transferred between the ARM and memory efficiently. There may be occasions, though, when you want to store a signed number in a single byte, i.e. -128 to 127, instead of more usual 0..255. Now **LDRB** performs a zero-extension on the byte, i.e. bits 8..31 of the destination are set to 0 automatically. This means that when loaded, a signed byte will have its range changed to 0..255. To sign extend a byte loaded from memory, preserving its signed range, this sequence may be used:

```
LDRB    R0,  <address>       ;Load the byte
MOV     R0,  R0,  LSL #24    ;Move to bits 24..31
MOV     R0,  R0,  ASR #24    ;Move back with sign
```

It works by shifting the byte to the most significant byte of the register, so that the sign bit of the byte (bit 7) is at the sign bit of the word (bit 31). The arithmetic shift right then moves the byte back again, extending the sign as it does so. After this, normal 32-bit ARM instructions may be performed on the word.

(If you are sceptical about this technique giving the correct signed result, consider eight-bit and 32-bit two's complement representation of numbers. If you examine a negative number, zero and a positive number, you will see that in all cases, bit 7 of the eight-bit version is the same as bits 8..31 of the 32-bit representation.)

The store operation doesn't need any special attention: **STRB** will just store bits 0..7 of the word, and bit 7 will be the sign bit (assuming, of course, that the signed 32-bit number being stored is in the range -128..+127 which a single byte can represent).

Double-byte (16-bit) operands are best accessed using a couple of **LDRB**s or **STRB**s. To load an unsigned 16-bit operand from an byte-aligned address use:

```
LDRB    R0,  <address>
LDRB    R1,  <address>+1
ORR     R0,  R0,  R1,  LSL  #8
```

The calculation of **<address>+1** might require an extra instruction, but if the address of the two-byte value is stored in a base register, pre- or post-indexing with an immediate offset could be used:

```
LDRB    R0,  [addr,  #0]
LDRB    R1,  [addr,  #1]
ORR     R0,  R0,  R1,  LSL  #8
```

Extending the sign of a two-byte value is similar to the method given for single bytes shown above, but the shifts are only by 16 bits.

To store a sixteen-bit quantity at an arbitrary byte position also requires three instructions:

```
STRB    R0,  <address>
MOV     R0,  R0,  ROR  #8
STRB    R0,  <address>+1
```

We use **ROR #8** to obtain bits 8..15 in the least significant byte of R0. The number can then be restored if necessary using:

```
MOV     R0,  R0,  ROR  #24
```

Multiplication and division

Operations on integers are many and varied. The group one instructions cover a good set of them, but an obvious omission is division. Also, although there is a **MUL** instruction, it is limited to results which fit in a single 32-bit register. Sometimes a 'double precision' multiply, with a 64-bit result, is needed.

Below we present a 64-bit multiplication routine and a division procedure. First, though, let's look at the special case of multiplying a register by a constant. There are several simple cases we can spot immediately. Multiplication by a power of two is simply a matter of shifting the register left by that number of places. For example, to obtain R0*16, we would use:

```
MOV     R0, R0, ASL #4
```

as $16=2^4$. This will work just as well for a negative number as a positive one, as long as the result can be represented in 32-bit two's complement. Multiplication by 2^n-1 or 2^n+1 is just as straightforward:

```
RSB     R0, R0, R0, ASL #n     ;R0=R0*(2^n-1)
ADD     R0, R0, R0, ASL #n     ;R0=R0*(2^n+1)
```

So, to multiply R0 by 31 ($=2^5-1$) and again by 5 ($=2^2+1$) we would use:

```
RSB     R0, R0, R0, ASL #5
ADD     R0, R0, R0, ASL #2
```

Other numbers can be obtained by factorising the multiplier and performing several shift operations. For example, to multiply by 10 we would multiply by 2 then by 5:

```
MOV     R0, R0, R0, ASL #1
ADD     R0, R0, R0, ASL #2
```

You can usually spot by inspection the optimum sequence of shift instructions to multiply by a small constant.

Now we present a routine which multiplies one register by another and produces a 64-bit result in two other registers. The registers **lhs** and **rhs** are the two source operands and **dest** and **dest+1** are the destination registers. We also require a register **tmp** for storing temporary results.

The routine works by dividing the task into four separate multiplies. The biggest numbers that **MUL** can handle without overflow are two 16-bit operands. Thus if we split each of our 32-bit registers into two halves, we have to perform:-

```
lhs (low) * rhs (low)
lhs (low) * rhs (high)
lhs (high) * rhs (low)
lhs (high) * rhs (high)
```

These four products then have to be combined in the correct way to produce the final result. Here is the routine, with thanks to Acorn for permission to reproduce it.

```
;
; 32 X 32 bit multiply.
; Source operands in lhs, rhs
; result in dest, dest+1
; tmp is a working register
;
.mul64
    MOV      tmp, lhs, LSR #16      ;Get top 16 bits of lhs
    MOV      dest+1, rhs, LSR #16   ;Get top 16 bits of rhs
    BIC      lhs,lhs,tmp,LSL #16    ;Clear top 16 bits of lhs
    BIC      rhs,rhs,dest+1,LSL#16  ;Clear top 16 bits of rhs
    MUL      dest, lhs, rhs         ;Bits 0-15 and 16-31
    MUL      rhs, tmp, rhs          ;Bits 16-47, part 1
    MUL      lhs, dest+1, lhs       ;Bits 16-47, part 2
    MUL      dest+1, tmp, dest+1    ;Bits 32-63
    ADDS     lhs, rhs, lhs          ;Add the two bits 16-47
    ADDCS    dest+1, dest+1, #&10000 ;Add in carry from above
    ADDS     dest, dest, lhs, LSL #16 ;Final bottom 32 bits
    ADC      dest+1,dest+1,lhs,LSR#16 ;Final top 32 bits
```

The worst times for the four **MUL**s are 8 s-cycles each. This leads to an overal worst-case timing of 40 s-cycles for the whole routine, or 5us on an 8MHz ARM.

The division routine we give is a 32-bit by 32-bit signed divide, leaving a 32-bit result and a 32-bit remainder. It uses an unsigned division routine to do most of the work. The algorithm for the unsigned divide works as follows. The quotient (**div**) and remainder (**mod**) are set to zero, and a count initialised to 32. The **lhs** is shifted until its first 1 bit occupies bit 31, or the count reaches zero. In the latter case, **lhs** was zero, so the routine returns straightaway.

For the remaining iterations, the following occurs. The top bit of **lhs** is shifted into the bottom of **mod**. This forms a value from which a 'trial subtract' of the **rhs** is done. If this subtract would yield a negative result, **mod** is too small, so the next bit of **lhs** is shifted in and a 0 is shifted into the quotient. Otherwise, the subtraction is performed, and the remainder from this left in **mod**, and a 1 is shifted into the quotient. When the count is exhausted, the remainder from the division will be left in **mod**, and the quotient will be in **div**.

In the signed routine, the sign of the result is the product of the signs of the operands (i.e. plus for same sign, minus for different) and the sign of the remainder is the sign of the left hand side. This ensures that the remainder always complies with the formula:

```
a MOD b = a - b*(a DIV b)
```

The routine is listed below:

```
DIM org 200
lhs = 0
rhs = 1
div = 2
mod = 3
divSgn = 4
modSgn = 5
count = 6
sp = 13
link = 14
FOR pass=0 TO 2 STEP 2
P%=org
[ opt pass
;
;sDiv32. 32/32 bit signed division/remainder
;Arguments in lhs and rhs. Uses the following registers:
;divSgn, modSgn - The signs of the results
;count - bit count for main loop
;div -    holds lhs / rhs on exit, truncated result
;mod -    hold lhs mod rhs on exit
;
.sDiv32
    STMFD   (sp)!, {link}
    EORS    divSgn, lhs, rhs        ;Get sign of div
    MOVS    modSgn, lhs             ;and of mod
    RSBMI   lhs, lhs, #0            ;Make positive
    TEQ     rhs, #0                 ;Make rhs positive
    RSBMI   rhs, rhs, #0
    BL      uDiv32                  ;Do the unsigned div
    TEQ     divSgn, #0              ;Get correct signs
    RSBMI   div, div, #0
    TEQ     modSgn, #0              ;and of mod
    RSBMI   mod, mod, #0
;
;This is just so the BASIC program can
;read the results after the call
;
    ADR     count, result
    STMIA   count, {div,mod}
    LDMFD   (sp)!,{pc}              ;Return
;
.uDiv32
    TEQ     rhs, #0                 ;Trap div by zero
    BEQ     divErr
```

```
    MOV     mod, #0                 ;Init remainder
    MOV     div, #0                 ;and result
    MOV     count, #32              ;Set up count
.divLp1
    SUBS    count, count, #1        ;Get first 1 bit of lhs
    MOVEQ   pc, link                ;into bit 31. Return if 0
    MOVS    lhs, lhs, ASL #1
    BPL     divLp1
.divLp2
    MOVS    lhs, lhs, ASL #1        ;Get next bit into...
    ADC     mod, mod, mod           ;mod for trial subtract
    CMP     mod, rhs                ;Can we subtract?
    SUBCS   mod, mod, rhs           ;Yes, so do
    ADC     div, div, div           ;Shift carry into result
    SUBS    count, count, #1        ;Next loop
    BNE     divLp2
.divErr
    MOV     pc, link                ;Return
;
.result
    EQUD  0
    EQUD  0
]
NEXT pass
@%=&0A0A
FOR i%=1 TO 6
    A%=RND : B%=RND
    CALL sDiv32
    d%=!result : m%=result!4
    PRINTA%" DIV ";B%" = ";d%" (";A% DIV B%")"
    PRINTA%" MOD ";B%" = ";m%" (";A% MOD B%")"
    PRINT
NEXT i%
```

ASCII to binary conversion

Numbers are represented as printable characters for the benefit of us humans, and stored in binary for efficiency in the computer. Obviously routines are needed to convert between these representations. The two subroutines listed in this section perform conversion of an ASCII string of decimal digits to 32-bit signed binary, and vice versa.

The ASCII-to-binary routine takes a pointer to a string and returns the number represented by the string, with the pointer pointing at the first non-decimal digit.

```
DIM org 200
REM Register assignments
bin = 0
sgn = 1
ptr = 3
ch  = 4
sp = 13
```

```
link = 14
cr = &0D
FOR pass=0 TO 2 STEP 2
P%=org
[ opt pass
.testAscToBin
;Test routine for ascToBin
;
    STMFD  (sp)!,{link}      ;Save return address
    ADR    ptr,digits        ;Set up pointer to the string
    BL     ascToBin          ;Convert it to binary in R0
    LDMFD  (sp)!,{PC}        ;Return with result
;
.digits
    EQUS   "-123456"
    EQUB   cr
;
;ascToBin. Read a string of ASCII digits at ptr,
;optionally preceded by a + or - sign. Return the
;signed binary number corresponding to this in bin.
;
.ascToBin
    STMFD   (sp)!,{sgn,ch,link}
    MOV     bin,#0                  ;Init result
    MOV     sgn,#0                  ;Init sign to pos.
    LDRB    ch,[ptr,#0]             ;Get possible + or -
    CMP     ch,#ASC"+"              ;If +,just skip
    BEQ     ascSkp
    CMP     ch,#ASC"-"              ;If -,negate sign and skip
    MVNEQ   sgn,#0
.ascSkp
    ADDEQ   ptr,ptr,#1              ;Inc ptr if + or -
.ascLp
    LDRB    ch,[ptr,#0]             ;Read digit
    SUB     ch,ch,#ASC"0"           ;Convert to binary
    CMP     ch,#9                   ;Make sure it is a digit
    BHI     ascEnd                  ;If not,finish
    ADD     bin,bin,bin             ;Get bin*10. bin=bin*2
    ADD     bin,bin,bin,ASL #2      ;bin=bin*5
    ADD     bin,bin,ch              ;Add in this digit
    ADD     ptr,ptr,#1              ;Next character
    B       ascLp
.ascEnd
    TEQ     sgn,#0                  ;If there was - sign
    RSBMI   bin,bin,#0              ;Negate the result
    LDMFD   (sp)!,{sgn,ch,pc}
]
NEXT pass
PRINT "These should print the same:"
PRINT $digits ' ;USRtestAscToBin
```

Notice that we do not use a general purpose multiply to obtain **bin***10. As this is **bin***2*5, we can obtain the desired result using just a couple of **ADD**s. As with many of the routines in this book, the example above illustrates a technique rather than providing a fully-fledged solution. It could be improved in a couple of ways, for example catching the situation where the number is too big, or no digits are read at all.

To convert a number from binary into a string of ASCII characters, we can use the common divide and remainder method. At each stage the number is divided by 10. The remainder after the division is the next digit to print, and this is repeated until the quotient is zero.

Using this method, the digits are obtained from the right, i.e. the least significant digit is calculated first. Generally we want them in the opposite order - the most significant digit first. To reverse the order of the digits, they are pushed on the stack as they are obtained. When conversion is complete, they are pulled off the stack. Because of the stack's 'last-in, first-out' property, the last digit pushed (the leftmost one) is the first one pulled back.

```
buffSize=12
DIM org 200,buffer buffSize
REM Register allocations
bin = 0
ptr = 1
sgn = 2
lhs = 3
rhs = 4
div = 5
mod = 6
count = 7
len = 8
sp =13
link = 14
cr=&0D
FOR pass=0 TO 2 STEP 2
P%=org
[ opt pass
;
;binToAscii - convert 32-bit two's complement
;number into an ASCII string.
;On entry,ptr holds the address of a buffer
;area in which the ASCII is to be stored.
;bin contains the binary number.
;On exit,ptr points to the first digit (or -
;sign) of the ASCII string. bin = 0
;
.binToAscii
    STMFD  (sp)!,{ptr,sgn,lhs,rhs,div,mod,link}
    MOV    len,#0              ;Init number of digits
    MOV    mod,#ASC"-"
    TEQ    bin,#0              ;If -ve,record sign and negate
    STRMIB mod,[ptr],#1
    RSBMI  bin,bin,#0
.b2aLp
```

```
    MOV     lhs,bin             ;Get lhs and rhs for uDiv32
    MOV     rhs,#10
    BL      uDiv32              ;Get digit in mod,rest in div
    ADD     mod,mod,#ASC"0"     ;Convert digit to ASCII
    STMFD   (sp)!,{mod}         ;Save digit on the stack
    ADD     len,len,#1          ;Inc string length
    MOVS    bin,div             ;If any more,get next digit
    BNE     b2aLp
;
.b2aLp2
    LDMFD   (sp)!,{mod}         ;Get a digit
    STRB    mod,[ptr],#1        ;Store it in the string
    SUBS    len,len,#1          ;Decrement count
    BNE     b2aLp2
    MOV     mod,#cr             ;End with a CR
    STRB    mod,[ptr],#1
    LDMFD   (sp)!,{ptr,sgn,lhs,rhs,div,mod,pc}
;
;
.uDiv32
    STMFD   (sp)!,{count,link}
    TEQ     rhs,#0          ;Trap div by zero
    BEQ     divErr
    MOV     mod,#0              ;Init remainder
    MOV     div,#0              ;and result
    MOV     count,#32           ;Set up count
.divLp1
    SUBS    count,count,#1      ;Get first 1 bit of lhs
    MOVEQ   pc,link             ;into bit 31. Return if 0
    MOVS    lhs,lhs,ASL #1
    BPL     divLp1
.divLp2
    MOVS    lhs,lhs,ASL #1      ;Get next bit into...
    ADC     mod,mod,mod         ;mod for trial subtract
    CMP     mod,rhs             ;Can we subtract?
    SUBCS   mod,mod,rhs         ;Yes,so do

    ADC     div,div,div         ;Shift carry into result
    SUBS    count,count,#1      ;Next loop
    BNE     divLp2
.divErr
    LDMFD   (sp)!,{count,pc}
]
NEXT pass
A%=-12345678
B%=buffer
CALL binToAscii
PRINT"These should be the same:"
PRINT;A% ' $buffer
```

As there is no quick way of doing a divide by 10, we use the **uDiv32** routine given earlier, with **lhs** and **rhs** set-up appropriately.

6.5 Floating point

Many real-life quantities cannot be stored accurately in integers. Such quantities have fractional parts, which are lost in integer representations, or are simply too great in magnitude to be stored in an integer of 32 (or even 64) bits.

Floating point representation is used to overcome these limitations of integers. Floating point, or FP, numbers are expressed in ASCII as, for example, 1.23, which has a fractional part of 0.23, or 2.345E6, which has a fractional part and an exponent. The exponent, the number after the E, is the power of ten by which the other part (2.345 in this example) must be multiplied to obtain the desired number. The 'other part' is called the mantissa. In this example, the number is $2.345*10^6$ or 2345000.

In binary, floating point numbers are also split into the mantissa and exponent. There are several possible formats of floating point number. For example, the size of the mantissa, which determines how many digits may be stored accurately, and the size of the exponent, determining the range of magnitudes which may be represented, both vary.

Operations on floating point numbers tend to be quite involved. Even simple additions require several steps. For this reason, it is often just as efficient to write in a high-level language when many FP calculations are performed, and the advantage of using assembler is somewhat diminished. Also, most machines provide a library of floating point routines which is available to assembly language programs, so there is little point in duplicating them here.

We will, however, describe a typical floating point format. In particular, the way in which BBC BASIC stores its floating point values is described.

An FP number in BBC BASIC is represented as five bytes. Four bytes are the mantissa, and these contain the significant digits of the number. The mantissa has an imaginary binary point just before its most significant bit. This acts like a decimal point, and digits after the point represents successive negative powers of 2. For example, the number 0.101 represents 1/2 + 0/4 + 1/8 or 5/8 or 0.625 in decimal.

When stored, FP numbers are in normalised form. This means that the digit immediately after the point is a 1. A normalised 32-bit mantissa can therefore represent numbers in the range:

0.10000000000000000000000000000000 to
0.11111111111111111111111111111111

in binary which is 0.5 to 0.9999999998 in decimal.

To represent numbers outside this range, a single byte exponent is used. This can be viewed as a shift count. It gives a count of how many places the point should be moved to the right to obtain the desired value. For example, to represent 1.5 in binary floating point, we would start with the binary value 1.1, i.e. 1 + 1/2. In normalised form, this is .11. To obtain the original value, we must move the point one place to the right. Thus the exponent is 1.

We must be able to represent left movements of the point too, so that numbers smaller than 0.5 can be represented. Negative exponents represent left shifts of the point. For example, the binary of 0.25 (i.e. a quarter) is 0.01. In normalised form this is 0.1. To obtain this, the point is moved one place to the left, so the exponent is -1.

Two's complement could be used to represent the exponent as a signed number, but is is more usual to employ an excess-128 format. In this format, 128 is added to the actual exponent. So, if the exponent was zero, representing no shift of the point from the normalised form, it would be stored as 128+0, or just 128. A negative exponent, e.g. -2, would be stored as 128-2, or 126.

Using the excess-128 method, we can represent exponents in the range -128 (exponent stored as zero) to +127 (exponent stored as 255). Thus the smallest magnitude we can represent is $0.5/(2^{128})$, or 1.46936794E-39. The largest number $0.9999999998*(2^{127})$, or 1.701411834E38

So far, we have not mentioned negative mantissas. Obviously we need to represent negative numbers as well as positive ones. A common 'trick', and one which BBC BASIC uses, is to assume that the most significant bit is 1 (as numbers are always in normalised form) and use that bit position to store the sign bit: a zero for positive numbers, and 1 for negative numbers.

We can sum up floating point representation by considering the contents of the five bytes used to store them in memory.

byte 0	LS byte of mantissa.
byte 1	Second LSB of mantissa.
byte 2	Second MSB of mantissa.
byte 3	MS byte of mantissa. Binary point just to the left of bit 7. MS bit assumed to be 1, so mantissa sign stored in this bit.
byte 4	Exponent, excess-128 form.

Consider the number 1032.45. First, we find the exponent, i.e. by what power of two the number must be divided to obtain a result between 0.5 and

0.9999999. This is 11, as 1032.45/(2^{11})=0.504125976. The mantissa, in binary, is: 0.10000001 00001110 01100110 01100110 or, in hex 81 0E 66 66. So, we would store the number as:

byte 0	LSB	= &66
byte 1	2rd LSB	= &66
byte 2	2nd MSB	= &0E
byte 3	MSB = &81 AND &7F	= &01
byte 4	exponent = 11+128	= &8B

This are the five bytes you would see if you executed the following in BASIC:

```
DIM val 4            :REM Get five bytes
|val=1032.45         :REM Poke the floating point value
FOR i=0 TO 4         :REM Print the five bytes
    PRINT ~val?i
NEXT i
```

Having described BBC BASIC's floating point format in some detail, we now have to confess that it is not the same as that used by the ARM floating point instructions. It is, however, the easiest to 'play' with and understand.

The ARM floating point instructions are extensions to the set described in Chapter Three. They follow the IEEE standard for floating point. The implementation of the instructions is initially by software emulation, but eventually a much faster hardware unit will be available to execute them. The full ARM FP instruction set and formats are described in Appendix B.

6.6 Structured types

Sometimes, we want to deal with a group of values instead of just single items. We have already seen one example of this - strings are groups, or arrays, of characters. Parameter blocks may also be considered a structured type. These correspond to records in Pascal, or structures in C.

Array basics

We define an array as a sequence of objects of the same type which may be accessed individually. An index or subscript is used to denote which item in an array is of interest to us. You have probably come across arrays in BASIC. The statement:

```
    DIM value%(100)
```

allocates space for 101 integers, which are referred to as **`value%(0)`** to **`value%(100)`**. The number in brackets is the subscript. In assembler, we use a similar technique. In one register, we hold the base address of the array. This is the address of the first item. In another register is the index.

The ARM provides two operations on array items: you can load one into the processor, or store one in memory from the processor.

Let's look at a concrete example. Suppose register R0 holds the base address of an array of four-byte integers, and R1 contains the subscript of the one we want to load. This instruction would be used:

```
LDR     R2, [R0, R1, LSL #2]
```

Note that as R1 holds the index, or subscript, of the element, we need to multiply this by four (using the **LSL #2**) to obtain the actual offset. This is then added to the base address in R0, and the word at this address is loaded into R2. There is no **!** at the end, so R0 is not affected by write-back.

If the array was of byte-sized objects, the corresponding load operation would be:

```
LDRB    R2, [R0, R1]
```

This time there is no scaling of the index, as each item in the array occupies only one byte.

If you are accessing an array of objects which are some inconvenient size, you will need to scale the index into a byte offset before loading the item. Moreover, further adjustment might be needed to ensure that the load takes place on word boundaries.

To illustrate the problem of loading odd-sized objects from arbitrary alignments, we give a routine below to load a five byte floating point value into two registers, mant (the mantissa) and exp (exponent). The number is stored in memory as a four-byte mantissa followed by a single-byte exponent. An array of these objects could use two words each, the first word holding the mantissa and the LSB of the second word storing the mantissa. It would then be a simple job to load two words from a word-aligned address, and mask out the unused part of the exponent word.

Using two whole words to store five bytes is wasteful when many elements are used (e.g. an array of 5000 numbers would waste 15000 bytes), so we obviously have to store the numbers contiguously. It is quite likely, therefore, that the mantissa and exponent will be aligned in a way which makes simple **LDR** instructions insufficient to load the number into registers.

Consider the value stored starting at address &4001:

&4000   *****************
&4001   LSB of mantissa

&4002 2nd LSB of mantissa
&4003 2nd MSB of mantissa

&4004 MSB of mantissa
&4005 Exponent
&4006 ****************
&4007 ****************

Three bytes of the number are held in the three most significant bytes of one word; the last two bytes are stored at the start of the next word.

The technique we will use is to load the two words which the value straddles, then shift the registers appropriately so that **mant** contains the four bytes of the mantissa in the correct order, and the LSB of **exp** contains the exponent byte.

On entry to the code, **base** contains the base address of the array, and **off** holds the index (in elements rather than bytes).

```
    ADD     off, off, off, LSL #2;offset=5*offset
    ADD     base, base, off      ;base=base+5*n
    AND     off, base, #3        ;Get offset in bytes
    BIC     base, base, #3       ;Get lower word address
    LDMIA   base, {mant,exp}     ;Load the two words
    MOVS    off, off, LSL #3     ;Get offset in bits
    MOVNE   mant, mant, LSR off  ;Shift mantissa right
    RSBNE   base, off, #32       ;Get shift for exponent
    ORRNE   mant, mant, exp,LSL base ;OR in mantissa
.part
    MOVNE   exp, exp, LSR off    ;Get exponent is LSB
    AND     exp, exp, #&FF       ;Zero high bytes of exp
```

Notice we use **LDMIA** to load the two word. The code assumes that the register number of **mant** is lower than **exp**, so that the words are loaded in the correct order.

The last four instructions are all conditional on the byte offset being non-zero. If it is zero, the value was on a word boundary, and no shifting is required.

Arrays of strings

We have already noted that a string is an array of characters. Sometimes, we want an array of strings, i.e. an array of character arrays. For example, the BASIC declaration:

```
    DIM  name$(10)
```

gives us an array of 11 strings, **name$(0)** to **name$(10)**. How do we organise such a structure in assembly language? There are two solutions. If each of the strings is to have a fixed length, the easiest way is to store the strings contiguously in memory. Suppose we wanted ten strings of ten characters each. This would obviously occupy 100 bytes. If the base address of these bytes is stored in **base**, and the subscript of the string we want in **sub**, then this code would be used to calculate the address of the start of string sub:

```
ADD     base,base,sub,LSL  #3 ;Add  sub*8
ADD     base,base,sub,LSL  #1 ;Add  sub*2
```

After these instructions, **base** would point to (old) **base+10*sub**, i.e. the start character of string number **sub**.

Storing all the characters of every string can be wasteful if there are many strings and they can have widely varying lengths. For example, if a lot of the strings in an array contain no characters for a lot of the time, the storage used for them is wasted. The solution we present is to use an array of string information blocks instead of the actual characters.

A string information block (SIB) is a structure which describes the address and length of a string. Unlike the string itself, it is a fixed length, so is more amenable to storing in an array. BASIC uses SIBs to describe its strings. When you **DIM** a string array in BASIC, the only storage allocated is for the appropriate number of SIBs. No character storage is allocated until you start assigning to the strings.

The format of a BASIC SIB is:

bytes 0 to 3	address of the string
byte 4	current length of the string

When you **DIM** an array, all entries have their length bytes set to zero. As soon as you assign something to the string, BASIC allocates some storage for it and fills in the address part. The way in which BASIC allocates storage for strings is interesting in its own right, and is described in section 6.7

To illustrate how we might use an array of SIBs, the routine below takes a base address and a subscript, and prints the contents of that string.

```
DIM org 200
sub = 0
base = 1
len = 2
p1 = 3
```

```
p2 = 4
argPtr = 9 : REM BASIC's pointer to CALL arguments
WriteC = 0
sp = 13
link = 14
FOR pass=0 TO 2 STEP 2
P%=org
[ opt pass
;
;Print base$(sub) where base points to the start of
;an array of five-byte block of the format:
;  0..3 pointer to string
;  4 length of string (see section 4.7)
;and sub is the subscript 0..n of the desired
;string. The SIB may be at any byte alignment.
;
.pStr
;Get address of SIB = base+sub*5
   ADD     base,base,sub,LSL #2 ;base=base+sub*4
   ADD     base,base,sub        ;base=base+sub*1
   LDRB    len,[base,#4]        ;Get string len
   TEQ     len,#0               ;If zero,nothing to do
   MOVEQ   pc,link
;
;Arbitrary alignment load of four-byte pointer into
;p1. Address of pointer in base
;
   AND     sub,base,#3          ;Get offset in bytes
   BIC     base,base,#3         ;Get lower word address
   LDMFD   base,{p1,p2}         ;Load the two words
   MOVS    sub,sub,LSL #3       ;Get offset in bits
   MOVNE   p1,p1,LSR sub        ;Shift lower word
   RSBNE   sub,sub,#32          ;Get shift for high word
   ORRNE   p1,p1,p2,LSL sub     ;ORR in the high word
;
;Now print the string. NB len > 0 so we can test at the
;end of the loop
;
.pStrLp
   LDRB    R0,[p1],#1           ;Load a character into R0
   SWI     WriteC               ;Print it
   SUBS    len,len,#1           ;Decrememt the count
   BNE     pStrLp               ;Loop if more
.endPStr
   MOV     pc,link              ;Return
;
;testPstr. This takes a subscipt in sub (r0)
;and a BASIC string array CALL parameter
;and prints the appropriate string
;
.testPstr
   STMFD   (sp)!,{link}
   LDR     base,[argPtr]        ;Load the address of the
   BL      pStr                 ;CALL parm. Print the string
   LDMFD   (sp)!,{pc}
```

```
]
NEXT pass
DIM a$(10)
FOR i%=0 TO 10
    a$(i%)=STR$RND
NEXT i%
FOR i%=0 TO 10
    A%=i%
    PRINT"This should say "a$(i%)":      ";
    CALL testPstr,a$(0)
    PRINT
NEXT i%
```

Multi-dimensional arrays

A single list of items is not always sufficient. It may be more natural to store items as a table of two or even more dimensions. A BASIC array declaration of two dimensions is:

```
    DIM t%(5,5)
```

This allocates space for a matrix of 36 integers:

t%(0,0)	t%(0,1)	...	t%(0,5)
t%(1,0)	t%(1,1)	...	t%(1,5)
...	...	...	...
t%(5,0)	t%(5,1)	...	t%(5,5)

We can use such arrays in assembly language by imagining the rows laid out end to end in memory. Thus the first six words of the array would hold **t%(0,0)** to **t%(0,5)**. The next six would store **t%(1,0)** to **t%(1,5)** and so on. To calculate the address of **t%(a,b)** we use **base+a*lim+b**, where **lim** is the limit of the second subscript, which is 6 in this case.

The routine below takes **base**, **sub1** and **sub2**. It calculates the address of the required element, assuming each element is 4 bytes (e.g. an integer) and that there are 16 elements per row.

```
    ADD    sub1,  sub2,  sub1,  LSL  #4 ;sub1=sub2+16*sub1
    ADD    base,  base,  sub1,  LSL  #2 ;base=base+sub1*4
```

Once **base** has been calculated, the usual instruction could be used to load the integer at that address. In the more general case, the number of elements per row would be stored in a register, and a general multiply used to multiply **sub1** by this limit.

Bit fields

We end this discussion of the basic types of data by reverting to the lowest level of representation: the bit. We have seen how sequences of bits, usually in multiples of eight, may be used to represent characters, integers, pointers and floating point numbers. However, single bits may usefully store information too.

One binary digit can represent two values: 0 or 1. Often this is all we need to distinguish between two events. A bit used to represent a choice such as yes/no, true/false, success/failure is called a flag. We already know of several useful flags: the result flags in the status register. The V flag for example represents overflow/no overflow.

It is common to find in many programs a set of flags which could be grouped together and stored in a single byte or word. Consider a text editor. There might be flags to indicate insert/overtype mode, justify/no justify mode, help displayed/no help, case sensitive/insensitive searches. Each of these would be assigned a bit in the flag byte. The value given to a flag is that of the bit in that position. Thus we might define the examples above as:

```
insMode=   &01
juMode =   &02
hlpMode=   &04
snsMode=   &08
```

There are four main operations on flags: set, clear, invert and test. To set a flag, the **ORR** operation is used. For example, to set the **insMode** flag of register **flags**:

```
ORR     flags,  flags,  #insMode
```

Clearing a flag is achieved using **BIC**, bit clear. To clear both **hlpMode** and **snsMode**:

```
BIC     flags,  flags,  #hlpMode OR snsMode
```

To invert a flag we use the **EOR** operation. This is often called 'toggling a flag', because applying the operation repeatedly has the effect of switching the flag between the two values.

To invert the **juMode** flag:

```
EOR     flags,  flags,  #juMode
```

Finally, to test the state of a flag, we use **TST**. This performs an **AND** operation, and the result is zero if the flag is cleared, and non-zero if it is set:

```
    TST     flags,  #insMode
```

tests the insert mode flag. If you test more than one flag in a single **TST**, the result is non-zero if any of the flags are set, and zero if all of them are cleared. You can also use **TEQ** to see if all of a set of flags are set and the rest are cleared. For example,

```
    TEQ     flags,  #insMode  OR  juMode
```

sets the Z flag if **insMode** and **juMode** are set and **hlpMode** and **snsModer** are cleared. Otherwise Z is cleared.

As 32 bits are held in a single word, arrays of flags can be stored very efficiently. To illustrate this, we show *Byte* magazine's well-known Sieve of Eratosthenes program. This benchmark is often used to test the speed of a few simple types of operation, for example when various compilers for a language are being compared. The purpose of the program is to find prime numbers using a technique attributed to the eponymous Greek mathematician.

The Sieve technique works as follows. Start with an array of flags, one for each of the integers from 2 to the maximum prime to be found. All of the flags are set to 'true' initially, indicating that any number could be a prime. Go through the array looking for the next 'true' bit. The number corresponding to this bit is prime, so output it. Then go through all of the multiples of this number, setting their bits to 'false' to eliminate them from the enquiry. Repeat this process till the end of the array.

Byte's version of the Sieve algorithm is slightly different as it starts from the supposition that all even numbers (except for two) are non-prime, so they are not even included. For comparison, we give a BBC BASIC version of the algorithm first, then the ARM assembler one. The BASIC version is shown overleaf.

Each flag is stored in a byte, and the storage for the array of **size%** bytes is obtained using a **DIM** statement. Notice that the program doesn't actually print the primes it discovers, because the idea of the benchmark is to test the speed of things like array accesses, not printing. The place in the program where the prime would be printed is shown in a **REM**.

```
size%  =  8190
DIM  flags%  size%

count%  =  0

FOR  i%  =  0  TO  size%
     flags%?i%  =  TRUE
NEXT  i%
```

```
FOR i% = 0 TO size%
     IF flags%?i% THEN
        prime% = i%+i%+3 : REM PRINT prime%
        k% = prime%+i%
        WHILE k% <= size%
           flags%?k% = FALSE
           k% += prime%
        ENDWHILE
        count% += 1
    ENDIF
NEXT i%

PRINT count%
```

In the ARM assembler version, we are eight times more efficient in the storage of the flags, and use a single bit for each one. Thus 32 flags can be stored in each word of memory. The ARM version is shown below:

```
DIM org 2000
REM Register allocations
count = 0
ptr = 1
i = 2
mask = 3
base = 4
prime = 5
k = 6
tmp = 7
size = 8
iter = 9
link = 14
SIZE = 8190
iterations = 10
FOR pass=0 TO 2 STEP 2
P%=org
[opt pass
;Sieve of Eratosthenes in ARM assembler
;The array of SIZE flags is stored 32 per word from
;address 'theArray'. The zeroth element is stored at bit
;0 of word 0,the 32nd element at bit 0 of word 1, and so
;on. 'Base' is word-aligned
;
;Registers:
;   count  holds the number of primes found
;   mask  used as a bit mask to isolate the required flag
;   ptr  used as a general pointer/offset into the array
;   i  used as a counting register
;   size  holds the value SIZE for comparisons
;   base holds the address of the start of the array
;   prime  holds the current prime number
;   k  holds the current entry being 'crossed out'
;   tmp  is a temporary
;   iter holds the count of iterations
;
```

```
.sieve
    MOV     iter,#iterations
.mainLoop
    ADR     base,theArray
    MVN     mask,#0            ;Get &FFFFFFFF, ie all bits set
    MOV     size,#SIZE AND &FF;Load size with SIZE in 2 steps
    ORR     size,size,#SIZE AND &FF00
;
;Initialise the array to all 'true'. First store the
;complete words (SIZE DIV 32 of them), then the partial
;word at the end
;
    MOV     i,#SIZE DIV 32     ;Loop counter = number of words
    MOV     ptr,base         ;Start address for initing array
.initLp
    STR     mask,[ptr],#4 ;Store a word and update pointer
    SUBS    i,i,#1             ;Next word
    BNE     initLp
    LDR     tmp,[ptr]          ;Get last, incomplete word
    MOV     mask,mask,LSR #32-SIZE MOD 32 ;Clear top bits
    ORR     tmp,tmp,mask       ;Set the bottom bits
    STR     tmp,[ptr]          ;Store it back
    MOV     i,#0               ;Init count for main loop
    MOV     count,#0
.lp
    MOV     ptr,i,LSR #5       ;Get word offset for this bit
    MOV     mask,#1            ;Get mask for this bit
    AND     tmp,i,#31          ;Bit no. = i MOD 32
    MOV     mask,mask,LSL tmp
    LDR     tmp,[base,ptr,LSL #2]   ;Get the word
    ANDS    tmp,tmp,mask       ;See if bit is set
    BEQ     nextLp             ;No so skip
    ADD     prime,i,i          ;Get prime
    ADD     prime,prime,#3
    ADD     k,i,prime          ;Get intial k
    ADD     count,count,#1     ;Increment count
.while
    CMP     k,size             ;While k<=size
    BGT     nextLp
    MOV     ptr,k,LSR #5       ;Get word for flags[k]
    MOV     mask,#1
    AND     tmp,k,#31
    MOV     mask,mask,LSL tmp
    LDR     tmp,[base,ptr,LSL #2]
    BIC     tmp,tmp,mask                ;Clear this bit
    STR     tmp,[base,ptr,LSL #2]       ;Store it back
    ADD     k,k,prime                   ;Do next one
    B       while
.nextLp
    ADD     i,i,#1             ;Next i
    CMP     i,size
    BLE     lp
    SUBS    iter,iter,#1
    BNE     mainLoop
    MOV     pc,link            ;Return after iter iterations.
```

```
    ;
.theArray
]
REM  Reserve the bytes for the array
P%=P%+SIZE/8
NEXT
REM Time 10 iterations, as in Byte
TIME=0
primes = USR sieve
T%=TIME
PRINT"It took ";T%/100" seconds for ";iterations" loops."
```

Notice the sequence which obtains the mask and offset for a given bit in the array occurs twice. The first step is to find the word offset of the word which contains the desired element. There are 32 flags in a word, so the word containing flag **i** is **i DIV 32** words from the start of the array. The division by 32 is performed using a right shift by five bits. Next, the position of the desired flag within the word is needed. This is simply **i MOD 32**, which is obtained using **i AND 31** in the assembler. A mask, which starts off at bit 0, is shifted by (**i MOD 32**) places to the left to obtain the correct mask. Finally, to load the word containing the flag, a scaled indexed load of the form:

```
    LDR    reg,[base,offset,LSL #2]
```

is used, the **LSL #2** scaling the word offset which we calculated into a (word-aligned) byte address.

The difference in the speed of the BASIC and assembler versions is quite dramatic. BASIC takes 6.72 seconds to perform one iteration of the program. Assembler takes 0.73 seconds to perform *ten* of them, which makes it over 90 times faster. A version in assembler which more closely mirrors the BASIC version, with one byte per flag, takes 0.44 seconds for ten iterations.

6.7 Memory allocation

Some of the examples of ARM assembler we have already given rely on memory being available to store data. For example, strings are generally referenced using a pointer to the characters in memory, and arrays are treated in the same way. In a program that manipulates a lot of data, some way of managing memory must be provided. For example, a text editor needs to be able to allocate space to hold the text that the user types, and the BASIC interpreter needs to allocate space for program lines, variables etc.

The facilities provided by the operating system for the allocation of memory vary greatly from machine to machine. The UNIX operating system, for example, provides some useful 'library' routines for allocating a given number of bytes, freeing an area so that it can be re-used later, and extending an area already allocated. On the other hand, a simple operating system such as the environment provided by an ARM co-processor connected to a BBC Micro might just hand the program a large chunk of memory and leave the management of it entirely to the program.

In this section, we illustrate a simple way in which memory allocation may be implemented, assuming that the program is just handed a large 'pool' of space by the operating system.

Linked lists

In memory allocation, a structure known as the linked list is often found. A linked list of objects can be regarded as an array where the elements are not contiguous in memory. Instead, each element contains explicit information about the address of the next element. This information is known as the link field of the element. The last item in the list usually has a special link field value, e.g. zero, to mark it as the end, or may contain a link back to the first element (this is called a circular linked list).

Linked lists can be illustrated pictorially using boxes and arrows. For example, consider a linked list of items which contain two words of information in addition to the link. A list of them might be drawn like this:

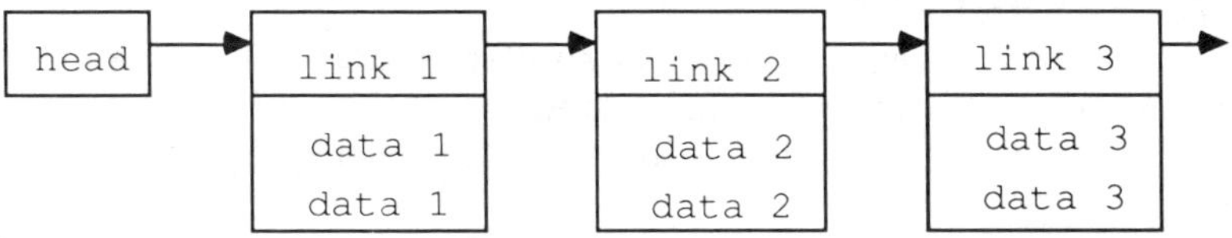

The 'head' is a pointer to the first element. This could be stored in a memory location, or in a register in the ARM. The first field in each element is the link pointer, and this is followed by two data words. The pointer for the third element does not point anywhere; it marks the end of the list.

There are many operations that can be performed on linked lists, and large sections of many books on algorithms and data structures are devoted to them. However, we are only interested in a couple of simple operations here: removing an item from the front of the list, and adding a new item to the front of the list.

To remove an item from the front, we just need to replace the head pointer with the link from the first item. When this is done, the list looks like this:

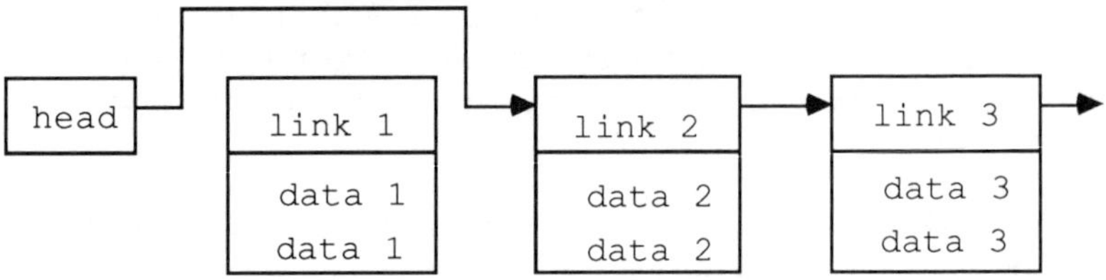

Notice that item number one is now inaccessible through the list, so in order to use it, a pointer to it must be 'remembered' somewhere. Notice also that if the item removed was the last one, the head pointer would be given the end of list value, and would not point at anything. This is known as an empty list.

To insert an item at the front of the list, two actions are required. First, the head pointer is copied into the link field of the item to be inserted. Then, the head pointer is changed to point at this new item.

With this simple level of understanding of linked lists, we can now describe how they are used in memory allocation schemes.

String allocation

The allocation scheme presented is very similar to the one BBC BASIC uses to allocate space for its string variables, and so is suitable for that type of application. Operations which a string allocator must perform are:

Allocate an area. Given a length in bytes, return a pointer to an area where this number of bytes may be stored.

Free an area. Given a length in bytes, and a pointer, free the area of memory so that it can be used by another string when required.

Strings in BBC BASIC may be between 0 and 255 bytes long. The allocator always works in terms of complete words, so strings may occupy between 0 and 64 words. Recall from the discussion of string information blocks earlier that the length is stored along with the address of the characters which make up the string. From this length byte, the number of words required to hold the string can be deduced:

```
words = (len-1) DIV 4 + 1
```

The area of memory BASIC uses for its string storage is called the heap. A word-aligned pointer, which we will call **varTop**, holds the address of the next free byte on the heap. The upper limit on the heap is set by the stack, which grows down from the top of memory.

A very simple memory allocation scheme using the heap would work as follows. To allocate n bytes, calculate how many words are needed, then add this to **varTop**. If this is greater than the stack pointer, SP, give a '**No room**' error. Otherwise, return the old value of **varTop** as the pointer to free space, and update **varTop** by the appropriate number of bytes. To free space, do nothing.

This scheme is clearly doomed to failure in the long run, because memory can never be freed, and so eventually **varTop** could reach the stack and a '**No room**' error be generated. To solve this, BASIC has a way of 'giving back' storage used by strings. There are 64 linked lists, one for each possible number of words that a string can occupy. When a request for n bytes is made, a check is made on the appropriate linked list. If this is not empty, the address of the first item in the list is returned, and this is removed from the list. If the list is empty, the storage is taken from **varTop** as described above. To free n bytes, the area being freed is simply added to the front of the appropriate linked list.

The algorithms for allocate, free and initialise are shown below in BASIC.

```
DEF  PROCinit
    EMPTY  =  0
    DIM  list(64)
    FOR  i=1  TO  64
        list(i)   =EMPTY
    NEXT  i
    varTop  =  <initial  value>
ENDPROC

DEF  FNallocate(n)
    IF  n=0  THEN  =0
    words  =  (n-1)  DIV  4  +  1
    IF  list(words)  <>  EMPTY  THEN
        addr  =  list(words)
        list(words)  =  !list(words)
    ELSE
        IF  varTop  +  4*words  >  SP  THEN  ERROR  0,"No  room"
        addr  =  varTop
        varTop  +=  4*words
    ENDIF
=  addr

DEF  PROCfree(n,addr)
    IF  n=0  THEN  ENDPROC
    words  =  (n-1)  DIV  4  +  1
    !addr  =  list(words)
    list(words)  =  addr
ENDPROC
```

The ARM assembler versions of these routines rely on a register called **workSpace**, which always contains the address of the start of a fixed workspace area. In this example, the first word of **workSpace** holds the current value of **varTop**, and the next 64 words are the pointers to the free lists. Another register, **heapLimit**, is assumed to always hold the upper memory limit that the allocater can use. Here are the ARM versions of the three routines.

```
heapSize = 1000
DIM org 600,heap heapSize-1
addr = 0
n = 1
offset = 2
words = 3
tmp = 4
heapLimit = 5
workSpace = 6
sp = 13
link = 14
NULL = 0
FOR pass=0 TO 2 STEP 2
P%=org
[ opt pass
;Init. Intialise the memory allocation system
;It initialises varTop and sets the 64 linked list
;pointers to 'NULL'
.init
    STMFD   (sp)!,{link}
    ADR     workSpace,ws        ;Init workspace pointer
    BL      getVarTop           ;Get varTop in tmp.
    STR     tmp,[workSpace]     ;Save it
    MOV     tmp,#NULL           ;Init the pointers
    MOV     offset,#64          ;Word offset into workSpace
.initLp
    STR     tmp,[workSpace,offset,LSL #2]
    SUBS    offset,offset,#1
    BNE     initLp
    LDMFD   (sp)!,{PC}          ;Return
;
;Alloc. Allocate n bytes, returning address of
;memory in addr, or EMPTY if no room
.alloc
    SUBS    words,n,#1              ;Return immediately for n=0
    MOVMI   addr,#NULL
    MOVMI   PC,link
    MOV     words,words,LSR #2              ;Divide by four
    ADD     words,words,#1                  ;Plus one
;Get pointer for this list
    LDR     addr,[workSpace,words,LSL#2]
    CMP     addr,#NULL                      ;Is it empty?
    LDRNE   tmp,[addr]                      ;No, so unlink
    STRNE   tmp,[workSpace,words,LSL#2]
    MOVNE   PC,link                         ;And return
```

```
;Empty list so allocate from varTop
    LDR     addr,[workSpace]
    ADD     tmp,addr,words,LSL #2        ;Check for no room
    CMP     tmp,heapLimit
    STRLT   tmp,[workSpace]          ;Update vartop and return
    MOVGE   addr,#NULL               ;Return NULL if no room
    MOV     PC,link
;
;free. Take a size (in n) and address (in addr)
;of a string, and link it into the appropriate
;free list.
.free
    SUBS    words,n,#1                   ;Return if for n=0
    MOVMI   PC,link
    MOV     words,words,LSR #2           ;Divide by four
    ADD     words,words,#1               ;Plus one
;Get current head pointer for this size
    LDR     tmp,[workSpace,words,LSL #2]
    STR     tmp,[addr]                   ;Store it in new block
;Update head to point to new block
    STR     addr,[workSpace,words,LSL #2]
    MOV     PC,link                      ;Return
;
;Set tmp to point to 'heap' area
;and set up upper limit of heap
.getVarTop
    ADR     tmp,heap
    ADD     heapLimit,tmp,#heapSize
    MOV     PC,link
;
.ws EQUD    0                        ;Slot for varTop pointer
]
REM Reserve space for 64 pointers = 256 bytes
P%=P%+256
NEXT pass
```

The way in which **varTop** is initialised depends on the system. In BASIC, for example, **varTop** is initialised to the value of **LOMEM** whenever a **CLEAR**-type operation is performed. **LOMEM** itself is usually set to the top of the BASIC program, but can be altered using an assignment. These three routines show that a relatively small amount of code can perform quite sophisticated memory allocation.

Summary

We have seen that most types of data may be loaded into ARM registers and processed using short sequences of instructions. Simple items may be stored along with the program, but only if the program is executing in RAM. ROM programs may only access fixed tables of data within the program area. Other data must be accessed through pointer registers, using memory allocated by the operating system. Data should be accessed in a position independent manner.

7. Non-user modes

In the previous chapters, we have restricted ourselves to discussing the ARM while it is operating in user mode. For most purposes, this is all that is required. For example, large ARM programs such as the BBC BASIC interpreter manage to function entirely in user mode. There are times, however, when a program must execute in one of the other modes to work correctly. In this chapter, we discuss the characteristics of the non-user modes.

7.1 Extended programmer's model

Register set

As described in Chapter Two, there are four modes in which the ARM may operate. The bottom two bits of R15 (called s1 and s0) determine the modes, as summarised below:

s1	**s0**	**Mode**
0	0	0 User (USR)
0	1	1 Fast interrupt (FIQ)
1	0	2 Interrupt (IRQ)
1	1	3 Supervisor (SVC)

When the ARM is in a non-user mode, its register set differs slightly from the user mode model. The numbering of the registers is identical, but some of the higher numbers refer to physically distinct registers in modes 1 to 3. The complete register model for all modes is shown overleaf. Each column shows the registers which are visible in mode 0, 1, 2 and 3 respectively.

The register names without a suffix refer to the user registers that we are used to dealing with. As the diagram shows, each of the non-user modes has at least two registers which are physically separate from the user mode ones. R14 is the link register, so all modes have their own link register, and R13 is traditionally used as the stack pointer, so each mode can have its own stack. FIQ mode has five additional private registers. These are provided so that important information may be stored in the processor for instant access when FIQ mode is entered.

In Acorn documentation, the term 'supervisor' modes is used to describe all non-user modes. We will adopt this convention for the rest of this chapter. Where the actual processor mode 3 is meant, the term SVC mode will be used.

Here is the extended programmer's model:

USER	FIQ	IRQ	SVC
R0	R0	R0	R0
R1	R1	R1	R1
:	:	:	:
R7	R7	R7	R7
R8	R8_FIQ	R8	R8
R9	R9_FIQ	R9	R9
R10	R10_FIQ	R10	R10
R11	R11_FIQ	R11	R11
R12	R12_FIQ	R12	R12
R13	R13_FIQ	R13_IRQ	R13_SVC
R14	R14_FIQ	R14_IRQ	R14_SVC
R15	R15	R15	R15

Instruction extensions

Although there are no instructions which can only be used in supervisor mode, the operation of some of the instructions already described in earlier chapters does alter slightly. These differences are covered for each instruction group below.

Group one

Recall that in user mode, only the N, Z, V and C bits of the status register may be altered by the data manipulation instructions. The two interrupt mask bits, F and I, and the mode bits S0 and S1, may be read, but an attempt to alter them is ignored.

In supervisor mode, all eight bits of the status register may be changed. In fact, the very act of entering a supervisor mode may cause a change in the state of the four special bits. For example when a **SWI** instruction is used to call a supervisor mode routine, S0 and S1 are set to decimal 3, i.e. SVC mode, and IRQs are disabled by the I bit being set.

The easiest way to set the F, I, S0 and S1 bits to a required state is to use the **TEQP** instruction. Recall that the instruction:

```
TEQP    pc,#value
```

performs an exclusive-OR of R15 (the PC and status flags) and the immediate value, but does not store the result anywhere. Because R15 is acting as a left-hand operand, only the PC bits (2 to 25) are used in the calculation, the status bits being set to 0. Furthermore, because the **P** option was specified after **TEQ**, the result of the exclusive-OR operation on bits 0, 1 and 26 to 31 of the operands is stored directly into the corresponding bits of R15. Thus the net result of the instruction is to store 1 bits in R15 where the **value** has one bits, and 0s where **value** was zero. You could view **TEQP** instruction as a special 'load status register' instruction of the form:

```
        LDSR    #value
```

As an example, suppose we are in SVC mode (S0 = S1 = 1) with interrupts disabled (I = 1), and want to move to FIQ mode (S0 = 1, S1 = 0) with both types of interrupts disabled (I = F = 1). The following instruction would achieve the desired result:

```
        TEQP    pc,#S0_bit + F_bit + I_bit
```

The following BASIC assignments would initialise the bit masks for the various status bits, such as **S0_bit**, used above:

```
S0_bit  = 1 << 1
S1_bit  = 1 << 2
F_bit   = 1 << 26
I_bit   = 1 << 27
V_bit   = 1 << 28
C_bit   = 1 << 29
Z_bit   = 1 << 30
N_bit   = 1 << 31
```

The **TEQP** instruction can only be used to store a given pattern of 1s and 0s into the status bits of R15. What we sometimes need is the ability to affect only some bits without altering others. This requires more work, as we have to read the current bits, then perform the desired operation. Suppose we want to disable both types of interrupts without altering the processor mode (i.e. F = I = 1, S0, S1 unchanged). Here is one way:

```
MOV     temp,pc                 ;Load current flags
ORR     temp,temp,#F_bit+I_bit  ;Set interrupt masks
TEQP    temp,#0                 ;Move new flags into R15
```

This time, the current flags' states are loaded into a temporary register using the **MOV** instruction. Remember that to read the status part of R15, it must appear as a right-hand operand in a group one instruction. The **ORR** is used to set the I and F bits without altering the others. Finally, the **TEQP** sets the status bits from temp.

As a final example, suppose we want to return to user mode (S0 = S1 = 0) without altering the rest of the flags. We could use the **TST** instruction to clear S0 and S1, leaving the other flags unaltered:

```
    MOV     temp,#N_bit+V_bit+C_bit+Z_bit+I_bit+F_bit
    TSTP    temp,pc
```

The **MOV** loads temp with a mask of the bits that are to be unaltered, and the **TST** does an **AND** of this and the current status register, putting the result in R15, as the **P** option is specified.

Group two

There is only one difference between using **LDR** and **STR** in supervisor mode and user mode. Recall that the post-indexed instructions of the form:

```
    LDR     <reg>,[<base>],<offset>
```

always use write-back, so there is no need to include a **!** at the end of the instruction to specify it. Well, the bit in the instruction code which would specify write-back is used for something else. It is ignored in user mode, but in supervisor mode it affects the state of a signal (called SPVMD, described below) which tells peripheral devices if the CPU is executing in supervisor or user mode.

Usually, when the ARM executes an **LDR** or **STR** in supervisor mode, the SPVMD signal tells the 'outside' world that this is a supervisor mode operation, so that devices like memory controllers can decide whether the requested data transfer is legal or not. If the **T** (for translate) option is given in an **STR**/**LDR** instruction, the SPVMD signal is set to indicate a user mode transfer, even if the CPU is really in supervisor mode. The **T** option comes after the optional byte-mode **B** flag, for example

```
    LDRBT   R0,[R1],#1
```

will load a byte into R0 addressed by R1, after which R1 will be incremented by one. Because **T** is present, the instruction will execute with **SPVMD** indicating user mode, even if the program is actually running in supervisor.

Note: The **T** option was included when it was envisaged that user and supervisor mode programs would have totally separate address spaces, with the former going through address translation and the latter not. As it turns out, the user address space enforced by the MEMC chip is actually a sub-set of the supervisor mode address space, so the **T** option is not usually needed. Remember also that its use is only valid with post-indexing, where the **!** option is not necessary.

Group three

The **LDM** instruction provides the ^ option. If present, this specifies that if R15 is loaded by the instruction, the status bits will be overwritten. If the ^ is absent, the status bits of R15 will be unaffected by an **LDM**, even if the rest of R15 is loaded. In user mode, only N, Z, V and C may be overwritten; in supervisor mode, all the status bits are affected.

In supervisor mode, the ^ option is relevant even if R15 is not in the set of registers being loaded. In this situation, its presence indicates that the user-mode registers should be loaded, not the ones relevant to the current mode. So, in FIQ mode, for example, the instruction

```
LDMFD   sp,{R0-R14}^
```

will load the user-mode registers from memory. However, if R15 was in the list of registers to be loaded, the instruction would have its usual effect of loading the registers appropriate to FIQ mode set, and the ^ would indicate that the status bits of R15 are to be loaded.

For **STM**, there is no corresponding need for ^, since all of R15 is always saved if specified in the register list. However, in supervisor mode, the presence of ^ in an **STM** is still relevant. Usually, an instruction like:

```
STMFD       sp,{R0-R15}
```

saves all of the registers which are visible in the current mode. For example, if the mode is SVC, then R0-R12, R13_SVC, R14_SVC and R15 are used. However, if ^ is specified, all registers saved are taken from the user bank, i.e. this instruction

```
STMFD   sp,{R0-R15}^
```

would cause R0-R15, all from the user bank of registers, to be saved.

Note that if write-back were specified in such an instruction, then the updated index register would be written back to the user bank instead of the appropriate supervisor mode bank. Therefore you should not specify write-back along with ^ when using the **STM** instruction from a supervisor mode.

Group four

The only difference between using branches in user and supervisor mode is that, in **BL**, the link register (R14) appropriate to the current mode is used instead of the user R14. This is as expected, and does not require any special attention.

Group five

When a SWI instruction is executed, the return address and flags are stored in R14_SVC. This means that when **SWI** is used from any mode other than SVC, no precautions are required to save R14 before the **SWI** is called. However, in SVC mode, executing a **SWI** will overwrite the current contents of R14_SVC. Therefore, this register should be preserved across calls to **SWI** if its contents are important.

To illustrate this, suppose a routine written to execute in user mode contains a call to the operating system's write character routine, but no other subroutine calls. It could be written thus:

```
;do some stuff
SWI     WriteC      ;Print char, R14_USR is preserved
;do some more stuff
MOV     pc,link     ;Return using R14
```

If the same routine is executed in SVC mode, the **SWI WriteC** would cause the return address in R14_SVC to be over written. The routine would have to be coded thus to work correctly:

```
STMFD   (sp)!,{link}   ;Save return address
;do some stuff
SWI     WriteC         ;Print char, R14_SVC is corrupt
;do some more stuff
LDMFD   (sp)!,{pc}     ;Return using stacked address
```

Memory map

We have mentioned previously that some ARM systems are fitted with a memory controller (MEMC) which, amongst other things, translates addresses emanating from the CPU, performing a mapping from logical addresses to physical addresses. It also controls the access to other devices, for example ROM and I/O. MEMC controls the access of various parts of the memory map, restricting the operations which can be performed in user mode. The SPVMD signal produced by the ARM CPU tells the MEMC if the ARM is in supervisor mode or not. This enables MEMC to enforce a 'supervisor mode only' rule for certain locations.

Recall that the bottom 32M bytes of the address space is allocated to 'logical' RAM. This is divided into pages of between 8K and 32K bytes, up to 128 of them being present. Each page has a 'protection level' associated with it. There are four levels, 0 being the most accessible, and 3 being the most restricted. When the processor is in user mode, pages with protection level 0 may be read and written; pages at level 1 may be read only, and levels 2 and 3 are inaccessible. In supervisor mode, all levels may be read or written without restriction. (There is also a special form of user mode, controlled by

MEMC, called OS mode. This allows read/write of levels 0 and 1 and reads-only of levels 2 and 3.)

The next 16M bytes of the memory map is set aside for physical RAM. This is only accessible in supervisor mode. The top 16M bytes is split between ROM and I/O. ROM may be read in any processor mode, but access to some I/O locations (e.g. those which control the behaviour of MEMC itself) is restricted to supervisor mode.

When an attempt is made to read or write an area of memory which is inaccessible in the current mode, an 'exception' occurs. This causes the processor to enter SVC mode and jump to a pre-defined location. There are various other ways in which user mode may be left, and these are all described below. Remember, though, that the memory scheme described in this section only refers to systems which use the Acorn MEMC, and might be different on your system.

7.2 Leaving user mode

There are several circumstances in which a program executing in user mode might enter one of the other modes. These can be divided roughly into two groups, exceptions and interrupts. An exception occurs because a program has tried to perform an operation which is illegal for the current mode. For example, it might attempt to access a protected memory location, or execute an illegal instruction.

Interrupts on the other hand, occur independently of the program's actions, and are initiated by some external device signalling the CPU. Interrupts are known as asynchronous events, because their timing has no relationship to what occurs in the program.

The vectors

When an exception or interrupt occurs, the processor stops what it is doing and enters one of the non-user modes. It saves the current value of R15 in the appropriate link register (R14_FIQ, R14_IRQ or R14_SVC), and then jumps to one of the vector locations which starts at address &0000000. This location contains a Branch instruction to the routine which will deal with the event.

There are eight vectors, corresponding to eight possible types of situation which cause the current operation to be abandoned. They are listed overleaf:

Vector	Cause	I F	Mode
&0000000	RESET	1 1	SVC
&0000004	Undefined instruction	1 X	SVC
&0000008	Software interrupt (SWI)	1 X	SVC
&000000C	Abort (prefetch)	1 X	SVC
&0000010	Abort (data)	1 X	SVC
&0000014	Address exception	1 X	SVC
&0000018	IRQ	1 X	IRQ
&000001C	FIQ	1 1	FIQ

The table shows the address of the vector, what causes the jump there, how the IRQ and FIQ disable flags are affected (X meaning it's unaffected), and what mode the processor enters. All events disable IRQs, and RESET and FIQ disable FIQs too. All events except the interrupts cause SVC mode to be entered.

Note that the FIQ vector is the last one, and the processor has no special use for the locations immediately following it. This means that the routine to handle a FIQ can be placed at location directly &1C, instead of a branch to it.

The following sections describe the interrupts and exceptions in detail. It is likely that most readers will only ever be interested in using the interrupt vectors, and possibly the `SWI` and undefined instruction ones. The rest are usually looked after by the operating system. However, fairly detailed descriptions of what happens when all the vectors are called are given. If nothing else, this may help you to understand the code that your system's OS uses to deal with them.

It is important to note that many of the routines entered through the vectors expect to return to the user program which was interrupted. To do this in a transparent way, all of the user's registers must be preserved. The PC and flags are automatically saved whenever a vector is called, so these can easily be restored. Additionally, all the supervisor modes have at least two private registers the contents or which are hidden from user programs. However, if the routine uses any registers which are not private to the appropriate mode, these must be saved and restored before the user program is restarted. If this is not done, programs will find register contents changing 'randomly' causing errors which are exceedingly difficult to track down.

7.3 RESET

The RESET signal is used to ensure that the whole system is in a well-defined state from which it can start operating. RESET is applied in two situations on most systems. Firstly, when power is first applied to the system, so-called power-on reset circuitry ensures that the appropriate levels are applied to the RESET signals of the integrated circuits in the computer. Secondly, there is usually a switch or button which may be used to RESET the system manually, should this be required.

On typical ARM systems, the MEMC chip, which contains the power-on reset circuitry, is used to control the resetting of the rest of the computer.

Upon receiving a RESET signal, the ARM immediately stops executing the current instruction. It then waits in an 'idle' state until the RESET signal is removed. When this happens, the following steps take place:

SVC mode is entered
R15 is saved in R14_SVC
The FIQ and IRQ disable bits are set
The PC is set to address &0000000

Although the program counter value when the RESET occurred is saved, it is not likely that an attempt will be made to return to the program that was executing. Amongst other reasons, the ARM may have been halfway through a long instruction (e.g. **STM** with many registers), so the affect of returning is unpredictable. However, the address and status bits could be printed by the operating system as part of 'debugging' information.

Likely actions that are taken on reset are initialisation of I/O devices, setting up of system memory locations, possibly ending with control being passed to some user mode program, e.g. BASIC.

7.4 Undefined instruction

Not all of the possible 32-bit opcodes that the ARM may encounter are defined. Those which are not defined to do anything are 'trapped' when the ARM attempts to decode them. When such an unrecognised instruction code is encountered, the following occurs:

SVC mode is entered
R15 is saved in R14_SVC
The IRQ disable bit is set
The PC is set to address &0000004

The program counter that is stored in R14_SVC holds the address of the instruction after the one which caused the trap. The usual action of the routine which handles this trap is to try to decode the instruction and perform the appropriate operation. For example the Acorn IEEE floating-point emulator interprets a range of floating point arithmetic instructions.

Having done this, the emulator can jump back to the user's program using the PC saved in R15_SVC.

By trapping undefined instructions in this way, the ARM allows future expansions to the instruction set to be made in a transparent manner. For example, an assembler could generate the (currently unrecognised) machine codes for various operations. These would be interpreted in software using the undefined instruction trap for now, but when a new version of the ARM (or a co-processor) is available which recognises the instructions, they would be executed in hardware and the undefined instruction trap would not be triggered. The only difference the user would notice is a speed-up in his programs.

7.5 Software interrupt

This vector is used when a `SWI` instruction is executed. `SWI` is not really an exception, nor is it a proper interrupt since it is initiated synchronously by the program. It is, however, a very useful feature since it enables user programs to call routines, usually part of the operating system, which are executed in the privileged supervisor mode.

When a `SWI` is executed, the following happens:

SVC mode is entered
R15 is saved in R14_SVC
The IRQ disable bit is set
The PC is set to address &0000008

As with undefined instructions, the PC value stored in R14_SVC is one word after the `SWI` itself. The routine called through the `SWI` vector can examine the code held in the lower 24 bits of the `SWI` instruction and take the appropriate actions. Most systems have a well-defined set of operations which are accessible through various `SWI`s, and open-ended systems also allow for the user to add his or her own `SWI` handlers.

To return to the user's program, the `SWI` routine transfers R14_SVC into R15.

7.6 Aborts and virtual memory

An 'abort' is caused by an attempt to access a memory or I/O location which is out of bounds to the program that is currently executing. An abort is signalled by some device external to the ARM asserting a signal on the CPU's ABORT line. In a typical system, this will be done by the MEMC, which controls all accesses to memory and I/O. Typical reasons for an abort occurring are attempts to:

write to a read-only logical RAM page
access physical RAM or I/O in user mode
access a supervisor mode-only logical page in user or OS mode
access an OS mode-only logical page in user mode
access a logical page which has no corresponding physical page

There are two types of abort, each with its own vector. The one which is used depends on what the ARM was trying to do when the illegal access took place. If it happened as the ARM was about to fetch a new instruction, it is known as a pre-fetch abort. If it occurred while the ARM was trying to load or store data in an **LDR/STR/LDM/STM** instruction, it is known as a data abort.

Virtual memory

Except for programming errors, by far the most common cause of an abort is when the system is running what is known as virtual memory. When virtual memory is used, not all of the program is kept in physical RAM at once. A (possible majority) part of it is kept on a fast mass storage medium such as a Winchester disk.

Suppose a computer is fitted with 1M byte of RAM, and it is required that a program 'sees' a memory space of 4M bytes. This 4M bytes might be located in the first part of the logical memory map, from address &0000000 to &003FFFFF. On the Winchester disk, 4M bytes are set aside to represent the virtual address space of the program. Now as only 1M byte of RAM is available, only a quarter of this virtual address space can be physically stored in the computer's RAM. In the diagram overleaf, the first 1M byte of the disk area is loaded into physical RAM and mapped into the lowest megabyte of the logical address space.

As long as the program only accesses instructions and data which lie in the first megabyte of the logical address space, a mapping into physical RAM will be found by the MEMC and no problems will occur. Suppose, however, that the program attempts to access logical address 2,000,0000. There is no physical RAM which corresponds to this logical address, so MEMC will signal this fact to the processor using its ABORT line.

The abort handler program responds to an abort in the following way. First, it discovers what logical address the program was trying to access. It then allocates a page of physical RAM which can hold the page of virtual memory corresponding to this address. The appropriate data is loaded in from the disk, and the logical to physical address map in the MEMC adjusted so that when the processor next tries to access the location which caused the abort, the newly-loaded data will be accessed.

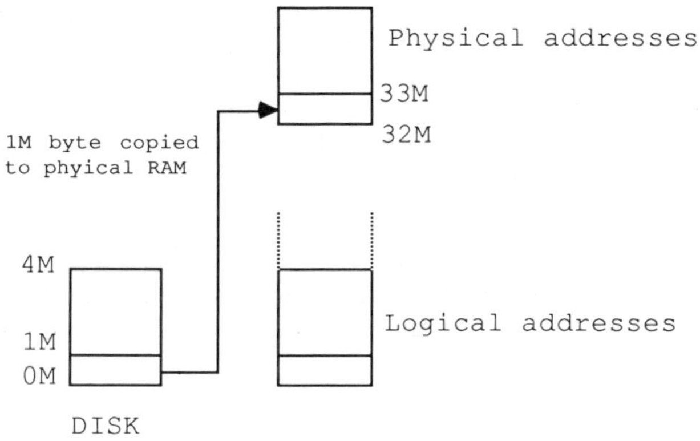

Now when a new page of virtual memory is loaded from disk, the previous contents of the area of physical memory used to store it must be discarded. This means that a range of addresses which used to be accessible will now cause an abort if an attempt is made to access them. Moreover, if that page contained data which has changed since it was first loaded from the disk, it must be re-written to the disk before the new page can be loaded. This ensures that the virtual memory on the disk is consistent with what is held in the RAM.

It is up to the software which deals with aborts to decide which page to discard when fetching a new page from the disk, and whether it needs to be written out before it is destroyed by the new data. (If the re-allocated page contain a part of the program, or read-only data, then it is not necessary to write it to the disk first, since the copy already stored there will be correct.) There are several algorithms which are used to decide the way in which pages are re-allocated in response to aborts (which are often called 'page faults'). For example, the so-called 'least recently used' algorithm will use the page which has not been accessed for the longest period of time, on the assumption that it is not likely to be required in the near future.

This may all seem incredibly slow and cumbersome, but in practice demand-paged virtual memory systems work well for the following reasons. Aborts are relatively infrequent as programs spend a lot of their time in small loops. ARM systems using MEMC have a fairly large page size (between 8K and 32K) so a program can spend a lot of its time in a single page without encountering 'missing' RAM. Additionally, virtual memory is often used on multi-tasking systems, where more than one program runs at once by sharing the CPU for short time slots. While the relatively slow transfer of data between RAM and disk is taking place, another program can be using the CPU. This means that although one program might be held up waiting for a segment of its virtual address space to be loaded from disk, another program whose program and data are in physical RAM can proceed.

The subject of virtual memory is a complex one which is covered in a variety of text books. A good one is 'The Design of the Unix Operating System' by MJ Bach, published by Prentice-Hall.

Pre-fetch aborts

When a pre-fetch abort occurs, the ARM completes the instruction(s) before the one which 'aborted'. When this instruction comes to be executed, it is ignored and the following takes place:

SVC mode is entered
R15 is saved in R14_SVC
The IRQ disable bit is set
The PC is set to address &000000C

The PC value saved is the one after the instruction which caused the abort. The routine which deals with the pre-fetch abort must perform some action, as outlined above, which will enable the instruction to be re-tried and this time succeed.

A simple single-tasking (one program at once) operating system running virtual memory might take the following steps on receiving a pre-fetch abort:

verify that it is a missing page problem (not access violation)
enable IRQs
find a suitable page of physical RAM
load the page corresponding to the required logical address
set-up MEMC to map the physical to logical page
re-try the instruction by jumping to R14_SVC minus 4

It is important to re-enable IRQs so that the normal servicing of interrupts is not disturbed while the new page is being loaded in. The third step may itself be quite involved, since a decision has to be made about which physical page is suitable for loading in the new section of the program and whether its current contents must be saved, as mentioned above.

Data aborts

A data abort is a little more complex, since the ARM is halfway through the instruction by the time the abort occurs. If the instruction was an **LDR** or

STR, it is abandoned and no registers are altered (in particular, the base register is unchanged, even if write-back was specified).

If the instruction was an **LDM** or **STM**, the instruction completes (though no registers are altered in an **LDM**), and the base register is updated if write-back was enabled. Note that if the base register was included in the list of registers to be loaded, it is not over-written as would normally be the case. The (possibly written-back) value is left intact. Then:

SVC mode is entered
R15 is saved in R14_SVC
The IRQ disable bit is set
The PC is set to address &0000010

This time, R14_SVC is set to the instruction two words after the aborted one, not one. The abort handler routine must take the following action. It must examine the aborted instruction to find out the type and address mode, and undo the affect of any adjustment of the base register due to write-back. It can derive the address of the data which caused the abort to occur from the base register, and perform a similar paging process to that described for pre-fetch aborts. It can then re-execute the instruction, by jumping to address R14_SVC minus 8 using an instruction such as:

```
SUB     pc,link,#8
```

The time taken to decode the instruction which caused the abort and perform the appropriate operations varies according to instruction type, number of registers (for **LDM/STM**), type of indexing (for **LDR/STR**) and whether write-back was enabled. Calculations made from typical abort-handler code result in times of between 20 s+41n-cycles for the best case and 121 s+36 n-cycles for the worst case. On an 8MHz ARM system, these translate into approximately 13.4us and 27.1us respectively.

7.7 Address exception

An address exception occurs if an attempt is made to access a location outside the range of the ARM's 26-bit address bus. This can be caused by the effective address (base plus any offset) of an **LDR/STR** instruction exceeding the value &3FFFFFF, or if the base register in an **LDM/STM** instruction contains a value greater than this.

Note that in the latter case, the exception will only occur if the base register is illegal when the instruction starts to execute. If it is legal for the first data transfer, and subsequently exceeds &3FFFFFF having been auto-incremented, no exception occurs. Instead the address 'wraps round' and subsequent loads or stores take place in the first few locations of the memory map.

Unlike the aborts described above, the address exception is detected internally by the ARM, and not by the assertion of a signal by some external device. Like data aborts, however, the incorrect instruction is abandoned or 'completed' as described above.

On detecting the address error, the ARM causes the following to take place:

SVC mode is entered
R15 is saved in R14_SVC
The IRQ disable bit is set
The PC is set to address &0000014

If it is required that the instruction be re-started after an address exception has been generated, the address in R14_SVC minus 4 can be used. However, there is usually not much point and the usual action is to enter a 'monitor' program which can be used to try to diagnose what went wrong.

7.8 IRQ

IRQ stands for Interrupt ReQuest, and is one of two interrupt inputs on the ARM. An external device signals to the ARM that it requires attention by asserting the IRQ line. At the end of every instruction's execution, the ARM checks for the presence of an IRQ. If an interrupt request has been made, and IRQs are enabled, the following happens:

IRQ mode is entered
R15 is saved in R14_IRQ
The IRQ disable bit is set
The PC is set to address &0000018

If IRQs are disabled, because the IRQ disable bit in the status register is set, the interrupt is ignored and the ARM continues its normal processing. Note that on initiating an IRQ routine, the ARM stes the IRQ, so further IRQs are disabled.

The routine handling the interrupt must take the appropriate action, which will result in the interrupting device removing its request. For example, a serial communications device might cause an IRQ when a byte is available for reading. The IRQ routine, on discovering which device caused the interrupt, would read the data byte presented by the serial chip, and buffer it somewhere for later reading by a program. The action of reading a byte from the serial chip typically informs the device that its IRQ has been serviced and it 'drops' the interrupt request.

On the ARM, the interrupt disable bits and processor mode bits in the status register cannot be altered in user mode. This means that user mode programs typically execute with both types of interrupt enabled, so that the 'background' work of servicing interrupting devices can take place. However, it is sometimes desirable to disable all interrupts, and there is typically a **SWI** call provided by the operating system which allows the interrupt masks to be changed by user mode programs.

The following few paragraphs refer to the writing of both IRQ and FIQ routines.

Interrupt routines must be quick in execution, because while the interrupt is being serviced, the main program cannot progress. The Acorn IOC (I/O controller) chip provides some support for dealing with interrupts which makes their processing more efficient. For example, it provides several IRQ inputs so that many devices may share the ARM's single IRQ line. These inputs may be selectively enabled/disabled, and a register in the IOC may be read to find which devices at any time require servicing.

An interrupt routine usually has limitations imposed on what it can do. For example, it is undesirable for an interrupt handler to re-enable interrupts. If it does, another IRQ may come along which causes the handler to be called again, i.e. the routine is re-entered.

It is possible to write code which can cope with this, and such routines are known as re-entrant. Amongst other things, re-entrant routines must not use any absolute workspace, and must preserve the contents of all registers that they use (which all interrupt routines should do anyway). The first restriction means that the stack should be used for all workspace requirements of the routine, including saving the registers. This ensures that each re-entered version of the routine will have its own work area.

Unfortunately, it is common to find that operating system routines are impossible to write in a re-entrant fashion. This means that it is not possible to use many operating system routines from within interrupt service code. A common example is to find that a machine's output character routine is executed with interrupts enabled and is not re-entrant. (The reason is that in some circumstances, e.g. clearing the screen, the output routine might take several milliseconds, or even seconds, and it would be unwise to disable interrupts for this long.)

You should consult your system's documentation to find out the exact restrictions about using OS routines from within interrupt service code.

Interrupt routines should also be careful about not corrupting memory that might be used by the 'foreground' program. Using the stack for all workspace is one way to avoid this problem. However, this is not always possible (for example, if the IRQ routine has to access a buffer used by the foreground program). You should always endeavour to restrict the sharing of locations by interrupt and non-interrupt code to a bare minimum. It is very hard to track down bugs which are caused by locations being changed by something outside the control of the program under consideration.

To return to the user program, the IRQ routine subtracts 4 from the PC saved in R14_IRQ and places this in R15. Note that this saved version will have the IRQ disable bit clear, so as well as returning to the main program, the transfer causes IRQs to be re-enabled.

7.9 FIQ

FIQ stands for Fast Interrupt reQuest. A signal on the ARM's FIQ input causes FIQ mode to be entered, if enabled. As with IRQs, the ARM checks at the end of each instruction for a FIQ. If both types of interrupt occur at the same time, the FIQ is handled first. In this respect, it has a higher priority than IRQ. On responding to a FIQ, the ARM initiates the following actions:

FIQ mode is entered
R15 is saved in R14_FIQ
The FIQ and IRQ disable bits are set
The PC is set to address &000001C

Notice that a FIQ disables subsequent FIQs and IRQs, so that whereas a FIQ can interrupt an IRQ, the reverse is not true (unless the FIQ handler explicitly enables IRQs).

The term 'fast' for this type of interrupt is derived from a couple of its properties. First, FIQ mode has more 'private' registers than the other supervisor modes. This means that in order for a FIQ routine to do its job, it has to spend less time preserving any user registers that it uses than an IRQ routine would. Indeed, it is common for a FIQ routine not to use any user registers at all, the private ones being sufficient. Secondly, the FIQ vector was cleverly made the last one. This means that there is no need to have a branch instruction at address &000001C. Instead, the routine itself can start there, saving valuable microseconds (or fractions thereof).

To return to the user program, the FIQ routine subtracts 4 from the PC saved in R14_FIQ and places this in R15 (i.e. the PC). Note that this saved version will have the FIQ disable bit clear, so as well as returning to the interrupted program, the transfer causes FIQs to be re-enabled.

Appendix A The Co-processor Instructions

In Chapter Seven, we talked about the undefined instruction trap. This occurs when the ARM tries to execute an instruction which does not have a valid interpretation. There are over four billion possible combinations of the 32 bits which form an instruction code, so it is not really surprising that some of these are not defined to do anything meaningful.

There are two types of undefined instruction. The first set are totally illegal, and cause the undefined instruction vector to be called whenever they are encountered. The second set are only classed as illegal if there is no co-processor in the system which can execute them. Unsurprisingly, these are called the co-processor instructions. Note that the ARM itself treats all undefined instructions as possible co-processor ones. The only thing which distinguishes the first class from the second is that no co-processor will ever indicate that it can execute the first type.

Note also that if an instruction is not executed because its condition codes cause it to be ignored by the ARM, it will never be 'offered' to a co-processor, or trapped as an undefined instruction. This means that if an instruction is a 'no-operation' due to its condition code being 'never', the rest of instruction can be anything - it will never cause a trap to occur.

A.1 ARM/co-processor handshaking

An ARM co-processor is an external chip (or chips), connected to the ARM data and control buses. When the ARM fails to recognise an instruction, it initiates a co-processor handshake sequence, using three special signals which connect the two chips together. The three signals are:

CPI Co-processor instruction.

The ARM asserts this when it encounters any undefined instruction. All co-processors in the system monitor it, ready to leap into action when they see it become active.

CPA Co-processor absent.

When a co-processor sees that an undefined instruction has been fetched (by reading the CPI signal), it uses CPA to tell the ARM if it can execute it. There are two parts to the instruction which determine whether it is 'co-processable'. The first is a single bit which indicates whether a particular undefined instruction is a proper co-processor one (the bit is set) or an undefined one (the bit is clear).

The second part is the co-processor id. This is a four-bit field which determines which of 16 possible co-processors the instruction is aimed at. If this field matches the co-processor's id, *and* the instruction is a true co-processor one, the co-processor lets the ARM know by setting the CPA signal low. If none of the co-processors recognises the id, or there aren't any, the CPA line will remain in its normal high state, and the ARM will initiate an undefined instruction trap.

CPB Co-processor busy

Once a co-processor claims an instruction, the ARM must wait for it to become available to actually execute it. This is necessary because the co-processor might still be in the middle of executing a previous undefined instruction. The ARM waits for the co-processor to become ready by monitoring CPB. This is high while the co-processor is tied up performing some internal operation, and is taken low when it is ready to accept the new instruction.

Note that while the ARM is waiting for CPB to go low, the program which executed the co-processor instruction is effectively halted. However, interrupts are still enabled, so these may be serviced as usual. When the interrupt routine returns to the co-processor instruction, it is effectively re-executed from the beginning, with the handshake starting again from the ARM asserting CPI. Note also that in a multi-tasking system, where several programs share the processor in turn, switching between tasks is performed under interrupts, so only the program which executed the co-processor instruction will be held up by the ARM waiting for the co-processor to become available.

Once the ARM gets the co-processor's undivided attention, they can execute the instruction between them. There are three classes of instruction, and what happens once the co-processor is ready depends on which class the instruction belongs to. Simplest are the internal co-processor operations. These require no further intervention from the ARM, which continues executing the next instruction, while the co-processor performs the required operation.

The second class is ARM to (or from) co-processor data transfer. This is where data is transferred between ARM registers and those on the co-processor. Thirdly, co-processor to (or from) memory operations may be executed. In these, the ARM provides the addresses, but data is transferred into or out of the co-processor. In the sections below, each class of co-processor instruction is described in detail.

Like the ARM, a co-processor can restrict instruction execution to supervisor mode only. It does this by monitoring the state of the SPVMD signal, described in Chapter Seven. If a privileged instruction is attempted from user mode, the co-processor could signal this using the ABORT line, just as the MEMC does. The abort handler code would have to be able to determine that it was a co-processor rather than the MEMC which created the abort, so that it could deal with it appropriately. However, there is no way in which an aborted co-processor instruction could be re-started, because the ARM cannot tell where the instruction originally came from.

A.2 Types of co-processor

Currently, only one co-processor's instruction set has been fully defined. This is the floating point unit (FPU). As the chips have not been made yet, even these instructions are treated as undefined ones. However, Acorn has written a program, the floating point emulator package, which intercepts the undefined instruction trap and emulates in software the floating point instruction set. The only difference between a system which has an FPU fitted and one which uses the emulator is the speed in which they execute the instructions (the emulator is anything between 10 and 100 times slower, depending on the operation).

Because of the way in which the co-processor protocol works, it is possible to design chips which recognise successively more of the instruction set. Thus a first generation FPU might just execute the four simple arithmetic operations in hardware, leaving the emulator to do the difficult stuff (possible using the FPU instructions to do it). A final version could implement the whole of the instruction set, leaving the emulator with nothing to do.

The FPU instruction set is described in Appendix B.

Further co-processors might concentrate on other aspects of a system. For example, a graphics co-processor might execute line-drawing and shape filling instructions, performing the required calculations and data transfers without placing any burden on the ARM. Such a chip would probably have its own screen memory so that it would not have to compete with the ARM for access to RAM.

A.3 Co-processor data instructions

This class of instruction requires no further action from the ARM once it has ascertained that there is a co-processor capable of dealing with it. However, as mentioned above, the ARM may still have to wait for the co-processor to become available before it can carry on with the next instruction.

Because there is no further communication between the ARM and the co-processor, the latter could incorporate an internal buffer where it stores the instructions for later execution. As long as there is room in the buffer (commonly called a FIFO for 'first-in, first-out queue'), the co-processor can accept an instruction immediately. Thus while the ARM is fetching and executing (defined) instructions from memory, the co-processor could meanwhile be executing its internal operations in parallel. This is similar to the well known Acorn Second Processor concept, where an I/O processor accepts commands from a FIFO while the language processor works independently on some other task.

In practice the amount of parallel processing which can be achieved is limited by the fact that eventually the ARM will want a result from the co-processor; so it will hang around waiting for the queue of instructions to be executed before it can ask for the required values. In situations where results are not required, e.g. a graphics co-processor which just takes commands and executes them without passing information back, the benefits can be great.

The general mnemonic for this type of instruction is **CDP**, for co-processor data processing. There are five operands which define which co-processor is required, which operation is required, which are the source and destination registers, and one for 'optional extra' information. Of course, the condition code mnemonic may also be present.

Here is the general form of a **CDP** instruction:

```
CDP{cond}  <cp#>,<op>,<dest>,<lhs>,<rhs>,{info}
```

Where:

{cond}	is the optional condition code
<cp#>	is the co-processor number (0-15)
<op>	is the desired operation code (0-15)
<dest>	is the co-processor destination register (0-15)
<lhs> and	
<rhs>	are the co-processor source registers (0-15)
{info}	is the optional additional information field (0-7)

The last five are all stored as four-bit (or three-bit in the case of **info**) fields in the instruction code. Note that except for the co-processor number field, which must be in a fixed place in the instruction for the system to work, none of the items has to be interpreted as above. A co-processor can place whatever meaning on the remaining 19 bits that it wants, but this standard defined by Acorn should at least be used as a starting point.

A particular type of co-processor would have its co-processor field value fixed, and the operation code could be given a more meaningful name. For example, the FPU has a **<cp#>** of 1 and uses the **<op>** field to describe one of sixteen possible instructions.

There are only eight registers in the FPU, so the top bit of the **<dest>**, **<lhs>** and **<rhs>** fields can be used for other purposes. For example, the top bit of the **<dest>** field is used to indicate which class of operation is required (dyadic, operating on two values, or monadic, operating on one).

So, although the FPU conforms to the spirit of the standard, it uses the fields to maximise the use of the bits available in the instruction. A typical FPU instruction is:

```
ADF {cond}<P>{R}   <dest>,<lhs>,<rhs>
```

where:
<P> is the precision of the operation
{R} is the optional rounding mode and the other fields are as above.

The **<P>** and **{R}** fields are encoded into the 'optional extra' information field and the top bit of the **<lhs>** field. For more details about the FPU instruction set, see Appendix B.

As another example, a graphics co-processor might use a **CDP** instruction to set its colour palette entries. For example,

```
CDP     2,<palette>,<entry>,<value>,<component>
```

where:
2 is the co-processor number
<palette> is the op-code for setting the palette
<entry> is the logical colour number (0-15) (the **<dest>** field)
<component> is the red, green or blue component (0-2) (the **info** field)
<value> is the intensity for that component (0-65535) (the **<lhs>** and **<rhs>**) field.

As long as the desired operation can be expressed in the number of bits available, any operation which requires no further communication between the ARM and co-processor can use a **CDP**-type instruction.

A.4 Co-processor register transfer operations

This class of co-processor instruction is used to transfer a single 32-bit value from the ARM to the co-processor, or from the co-processor to the ARM. The standard mnemonics are **MRC** for Move from ARM to Co-processor, and **MCR** for Move from Co-processor to ARM. The general forms are:

```
MRC{cond}  <cp#>,<op>,<ARM  srce>,<lhs>,<rhs>,{info}
MCR{cond}  <cp#>,<op>,<ARM  dest>,<lhs>,<rhs>,{info}
```

where:
<cp#> is the co-processor number (0-15)
<op> is the operation code required (0-7)
<ARM srce>/<ARM dest> is the ARM source/destination register (0-15)
<lhs> and **<rhs>** are co-processor register numbers (0-15)
{info} is optional extra information (0-7)

Notice that the number of possible opcodes has been halved compared to **CDP**, as there are now two directions between which to share the sixteen possible codes.

The **MCR** instruction does not necessarily have to be a simple transfer from a co-processor register to an ARM one. A complex internal operation could be performed on **<lhs>** and **<rhs>** before the transfer takes place. The co-processor only signals its readiness to the ARM when it has performed all the necessary internal work and is prepared to transfer the result to the ARM.

Again, the exact interpretation of the fields depends on the type of co-processor. An example of an FPU **MRC** operation is the 'float' instruction, to convert a 32-bit two's complement integer (in an ARM register) to a floating point number of some specified precision and rounding type (in an FPU register):

```
FLT{cond}<P>{R}   <ARM  srce>,<lhs>
```

Similarly, an FPU **MCR** instruction is the 'fix' operation, which converts a floating point number (in the FPU) to an integer (in the ARM):

```
FIX{cond}<P>{R}   <ARM  dest>,<rhs>
```

Notice that a different field is used in each case to specify the required FPU register. This does not concern the programmer, since only a register number (or name) is specified. It is up to the assembler to generate the appropriate binary op-code.

A graphics co-processor might use this instruction to read or write the current pixel location. If expressed as two sixteen bit co-ordinates, this could be encoded into a single 32-bit register. The operations might be:

```
MCR      2,<cursor>,<ARM  dest>
MRC      2,<cursor>,<ARM  srce>
```

In this case, only the opcode is set to **<cursor>** to indicate a cursor operation. The **<lhs>**,**<rhs>** and **{info}** fields are not used.

Using R15 in MCR/MRC instructions

When R15 in the ARM is specified as the **<ARM dest>** register, only four bits are ever affected: the N, Z, V and C flags. The PC part of R15 and the mode and interrupt bits are never changed, even in supervisor mode. This makes the **MCR** instruction useful for transferring data from the co-processor directly into the ARM result flags. The FPU's compare instructions use this facility.

If R15 is given as the **<srce>** register, all 32-bits are transferred to the co-processor. It is not envisaged that many co-processors will have a use for the ARM's PC/status register, but the ability to access it is there if required.

A.5 Co-processor data transfer operations

This group of instructions provides a similar function to the **LDR/STR** instructions, but transfers data between a co-processor and memory instead of between the ARM and memory. The address of the word(s) to be transferred is expressed in a similar way to **LDR/STR**, that is to say you can use pre-indexed and post-indexed addressing, using any of the ARM registers as a base. However, only immediate offsets are allowed, in the range -255 to +255 words (-1020 to +1020 bytes).

Like **LDR/STR**, write-back to the base register may be performed optionally after a pre-indexed instruction and is always performed after a post-indexed instruction.

The mnemonics are **LDC** to load data into a co-processor, and **STC** to store data. The full syntax is:

```
LDC{cond}{L}    <cp#>,<dest>,<address>
STC{cond}{L}    <cp#>,<srce>,<address>
```

where:
{L} is an optional bit meaning 'long transfer'; see below
<cp#> is the co-processor number (0-15)
<srce>,<dest> is the co-processor register number (0-15)
<address> specifies the address at which to start transferring data

Address modes

There are three forms that **<address>** can take: a simple expression, a pre-indexed address, and a post-indexed address.

If a simple expression is given for the address, the assembler will try to generate a PC-relative, pre-indexed instruction, without write-back. Thus if you say:

```
LDC     1,F1,label
```

(F1 being a co-processor register name) the assembler will generate this equivalent instruction:

```
LDC     1,F1,[R15,#label-(P%+8)]
```

assuming the label is after the instruction. Note that as with **LDR/STR**, the assembler takes pipe-lining into account automatically when R15 is used implicitly (as above), or explicitly (as below). Note also that the maximum offset in each direction is only 1020 bytes for **LDC/STC**, instead of 4095, which **LDR/STR** give you. If the address that the instruction tries to access is outside the available range, the assembler gives an error.

The remaining forms of **<address>** are:

[<base>]	address in ARM register **<base>**
[<base>,#<offset>]{!}	**<base>+<offset>**, {with write-back}
[<base>],#<offset>	**<base>**, then add **<offset>** to **<base>**

The offsets are specified in bytes, in the range -1020 to +1020. However, they are scaled to words (by dividing by four) when stored in the instruction, so only word-boundary offsets should be used.

These instructions differ from **LDR/STR** in that more than one register may be transferred. The optional **L** part of the syntax is designed to enable a choice between short (single word) and long (multiple word) transfers to take place. It is up to the co-processor to control how many words are transferred. The ARM, having calculated the start address from the base register, offset, and address mode will automatically increment the address after each operation.

Long transfers

Remember that **LDM/STM** always loads/stores registers in ascending memory locations. A similar thing happens with multiple register **LDC/STC** transfers. Suppose an **STCL** instruction for a given co-processor stores its internal registers from the one given in the instruction, up to the highest one, F7. The instruction:

```
STCL    1,F0,[R1,#-32]!
```

works as follows. The start address of the transfer is calculated from the contents of R1 minus 32. This is written back into R1. Then the eight data transfers take place, starting from the calculated address and increasing by four bytes after each one. Similarly,

```
LDCL    1,F4,[R1],#16
```

will load four registers, starting from the address in R1 and adding four after each transfer. Finally, 16 is added to the base register R1.

The FPU uses this group of instructions to load and store numbers from its floating point registers. There are four possible lengths allowed (single, double, extended and packed) which take one, two, three and three words of memory respectively. The **L** option only allows two possible lengths. However, the FPU only has eight internal registers, so the top bit of the **<dest>/<srce>** field is used to encode the extra two length options.

Apart from this minor difference, the FPU load and store data instructions obey exactly the general form of the co-processor data transfer, as Appendix B describes.

Aborts and address exceptions

Since this class of instruction uses the ARM address bus, instruction aborts and address exceptions can occur as for **LDM/STM** etc. In the case of an exception (the start address has one or more of bits 26-31 set), exactly the same action occurs as for a native ARM exception, i.e. the instruction is stopped and the address exception vector called. In the case of multiple word transfers, only an illegal start address will be recognised; if it subsequently gets incremented to an illegal value, it will 'wrap-around' into the first few words of memory.

Data aborts also behave in a similar way to native ARM instructions. As usual, if write-back was specified, the base register will be updated, but no other changes will take place in the ARM or co-processor registers. This enables the abort handler code to re-start the instruction after undoing any indexing. Note that it is up to the co-processor to monitor the ABORT signal and stop processing when it is activated.

A.6 Co-processor instruction timings

In addition to the n, i and i-cycles mentioned at the end of Chapter Three, co-processor instructions also use c (for co-processor) cycles. These are the same period as s and i-cycles.

CDP timing

1 s + B i-cycles.

MRC timing

1 s + B i + 1 c-cycles.

MCR timing

1 s + (B+1) i + 1 c- cycles.

LDC/STC timing

(N-1) s + B i + 1 c-cycles.

where:
B is the number of cycles the ARM spends waiting for the co-processor to become ready (which has a minimum of zero).
N is the number of words transferred.

Appendix B The Floating Point Instruction Set

Appendix A described the generic form which co-processor instructions take. In this appendix, we look at a specific use of these instructions: the floating point unit.

The definition given here does not describe any particular hardware. Rather, it gives a programmer's view of a system which could be implemented in a number of ways. In the first instance, the instruction set of the FPU has been implemented entirely in software. All of the instructions are trapped through the unimplemented instruction vector, and the floating point emulator package uses this facility to interpret the operation codes (using native ARM instructions) and perform the appropriate operations.

At the other end of the spectrum, a complete hardware implementation of the FPU would recognise the whole floating point instruction set, so the unimplemented instruction trap would never be used. The ARM's only involvement in dealing with the instructions would be in the generation of addresses for data transfers and providing or receiving values for register transfers.

The only difference, from the programmer's point of view, between the two implementations would be the speed at which the instructions are executed. The only reason for using a hardware solution is that this can provide a speed increase of hundreds of times over the interpreted implementation.

The FPU performs arithmetic to the IEEE 754 standard for floating point.

B.1 Some terminology

In describing the FPU's instruction set, we have to use certain terms which are specific to floating point arithmetic. These are explained briefly in this section. For a more detailed discussion, you should see the appropriate IEEE standard document (ANSI/IEEE 754-1985) , or manufacturer's data on one of the current available FPUs (e.g. the Motorola MC68881 or Western Digital WE32206).

Precision

The instruction set includes three precisions to which calculations may be performed. The precision of a floating point number is the number of digits which can be stored with total accuracy. It is expressed in bits. In Chapter Five, we talked about the mantissa of a floating number being the part which stored the significant digits, and the exponent being the scaling factor applied to it.

When we say a given floating point representation has n bits of precision, this means that the mantissa part is stored in n bits. The three standard IEEE precisions are 24 bits, 53 bits and 65 bits. These are known as single, double, and extended precision respectively. The mantissa is stored in one fewer bits than the precision implies because numbers are held in normalised form (as in BBC BASIC) and the MSB is an implicit 1. The binary point comes *after* this.

There is a fixed correspondence between the precision of a number expressed in bits, and how many decimal digits that number can represent. Mathematically speaking, an n-bit number can hold n*LOG(2)/LOG(10) decimal digits, or more simply, n*0.3010. Thus the three IEEE floating points types can accurately represent the following number of decimal digits:

Type	Precision	Decimal digits
Single	24	7.2
Double	53	15.95
Extended	65	19.6

Obviously you cannot have fractional numbers of significant digits, so the values should be truncated to 7, 15 and 19 respectively. The fractional part means that one extra digit can be stored, but this cannot go all the way up to 9.

There is one further form of representation for floating point numbers: packed decimal. In this form, the decimal digits of the mantissa and exponent are represented in a coded form, with four bits representing each decimal digit (only the combinations 0000 to 1001 being used). In this form, called packed decimal, the mantissa is stored as 19 four-bit 'digits', and the exponent as 4 four-bit digits.

Just because a number can be represented exactly in decimal, do not assume that its binary representation is also exact. For example, the decimal fraction 0.1 is actually a recurring fraction in binary, and can never be stored exactly (though of course, when enough digits are used in the mantissa, the error is very small).

Dynamic range

The mantissa has an imaginary binary point before after its first digit, and the first digit is always a binary 1, never 0. This is known as 'normalised form'. Thus the mantissa stands for a fraction between 1.0 and 1.99999... The exponent provides the power of two by which the mantissa has to be multiplied to obtain the desired value.

To obtain numbers greater than 1.999999... a positive exponent is used, and to represent numbers smaller than 1.0, a negative exponent is used (meaning that the mantissa is divided by a power of two instead of multiplied). The exact range of numbers depends on the maximum power of two by which the mantissa may be multiplied or divided. This is known as the dynamic range of the representation.

Each of the precisions uses a different size of exponent, as follows:

Precision	Exponent bits	Smallest	Largest
Single	8	2^{-126}	2^{127}
Double	11	2^{-1022}	2^{1023}
Extended	15	2^{-16382}	2^{16383}

The table shows how many bits the exponent uses, and the smallest and largest factors by which the mantissa may be multiplied. The formula n*0.3010 can also be used to find out what power of ten these exponents correspond to. They are +/-39, +/-307 and +/-4931 respectively. Thus a single precision IEEE number could represent the number 1.234E12 but not 1.234E45. This would require a double precision number.

The exponent is held in an excess-n format, as with BBC BASIC. The excess number is 127, 1023 and 16383 for the three precisions respectively. Note that there is an exponent value at each end of the range (e.g. -127 and +128, stored as 0 and 255, in single precision) which is not used. These values are used to represent special numbers.

Rounding

When the FPU performs its calculations, more digits are used than are necessary to store the numbers involved. Calculations are performed in what is called 'full working precision'. This is so that any errors which accumulate due to non-exact representations of fractions do not affect the final result. When a result is presented, the FPU converts the special full working form into a value of the desired precision. The way in which this conversion is performed is called the 'rounding mode' of the calculation, and there are four of them to choose from.

'Round to nearest' means that the final result is the closest number in the selected precision to the internal version. This is used as the default mode for ARM FPU instructions.

'Round to zero' means that the extra bits of precision are effectively ignored, so the final result is the one which is closest to zero.

'Round to plus infinity' means that the final result is the first number which is greater than the 'exact' result which can be stored in the required precision.

'Round to minus infinity' means that the final result is the first number which is less than the 'exact' result which can be stored in the required precision.

These four modes can be illustrated by using decimal numbers. Suppose that the calculations are performed to nine digits precision, and the final precision is seven digits:

Mode	'Exact' result	Rounded result
Nearest	0.123456789	0.1234568
	-0.123456789	-0.1234568
To zero	0.123456789	0.1234567
	-0.123456789	-0.1234567
To +infinity	0.123456789	0.1234568
	-0.123456789	-0.1234567
To -infinity	0.123456789	0.1234567
	-0.123456789	-0.1234568

Special values

In addition to valid numeric values, the IEEE standard also defines representations for values which may arise from errors in calculations. These values are 'not a number' (NAN), plus infinity (+INF) and minus infinity (-INF). There are actually two types of NAN, trapping and non-trapping. Trapping is described in the next section. The ways in which these special values may arise are also described there.

Note that IEEE defines two representations for zero, positive and negative zero. Usually the distinction between them is not important, but sometimes a result will depend on the sign of the zero used (see the DVZ trap below for an example).

B.2 Programmer's model

To the programmer, the FPU looks like a cut-down version of the ARM CPU. There are eight general purpose registers, called F0 to F7, a status register and a control register. There is no program counter; the ARM controls all interaction between a co-processor and memory. It is responsible for generating addresses for instruction fetches and data transfers.

Whereas the ARM's own 16 registers are 32 bits wide, there is no definition about how wide the FPU's registers are. The IEEE standard specifies several levels of precision to which operations may be performed, as described above. All the programmer needs to know about the FPU registers is that they are wide enough to maintain numbers to the highest precision required by the standard.

However, when floating point numbers are transferred between the FPU and memory, their representation becomes important. The formats of the various types of floating number are described in section B.6.

The FPU status register

The FPU's status register is 32-bits wide, and contains three fields. These are the status flags, the interrupt masks, and a system id field. There are five flags, and each of these represents a specific error condition which can arise during floating point operations. Each flag has a corresponding interrupt mask. When an error condition arises, the FPU checks the state of the interrupt mask for that error. If the interrupt is enabled, a trap is generated, which causes the program to halt. The appropriate status flag is set, so that the trap handler can determine the cause of the error.

If the interrupt for the error condition is disabled, the status flag still gets set, but execution of the program is not affected. A special result, e.g. NAN or INF is returned.

Note that the way in which an error interrupt is implemented depends on the system in which the program is executing. Software and hardware FPUs will have different ways of stopping the program.

The flags are set if the appropriate condition has arisen, and cleared if not. The masks are set to enable the interrupt, and cleared to disable it. There is an FPU instruction which is used to initialise the status register to a known state.

Here is the layout of the status register:

bit 0	IVO flag	
bit 1	DVZ flag	
bit 2	OFL flag	
bit 3	UFL flag	
bit 4	INX flag	
bits 5 to 15	Unused	(These are read as zero)
bit 16	IVO mask	
bit 17	DVZ mask	
bit 18	OFL mask	
bit 19	UFL mask	
bit 20	INX mask	
bits 21 to 23	Unused	(These are read as zero)
bits 24 to 31	System id	(These are 'read-only')

The meanings of the three-letter abbreviations are as follows:

IVO - Invalid operation. There are several operations which are deemed 'invalid', and each of these sets the IVO flag, and causes the instruction to be trapped if enabled. If the trap is not enabled, an operation which causes the IVO flag to be set returns NAN as the result. Invalid operations are:

Any operation on a NAN
Trying to 'cancel' infinities, e.g. -INF plus +INF
Zero times +INF or -INF
0/0 or INF/INF
INF **REM** anything or anything **REM** 0
SQT(<0)
Converting INF, NAN or too large a number to integer
ACS(>1), **ASN**(>1)
SIN(INF),COS(INF), TAN(INF)
LOG(<=0), LGN(<=0)
Writing to the unused or system id bits of the status register

where >1 means 'a number greater than one' etc, and INF means either +INF or -INF. Note that in the case of converting an INF or too large a number to an integer, the result (if the error is not trapped) is the largest integer of the appropriate sign which can be represented in 32 bits two's complement.

DVZ - Divide by zero. This is caused by trying to divide a non-zero number by zero. The result, if the error is not trapped, is an infinity of the appropriate sign (e.g. -1/0 gives -INF, -32.5/-0 gives +INF).

OFL - Overflow. This occurs when a result is being rounded to the specified precision for the operation. If it is impossible to legally represent the number, a trap occurs. If the trap is disabled, the result depends on the rounding mode specified in the operation:

Nearest	Appropriately signed INF
To zero	Largest representable number of appropriate sign
To +INF	Negative overflows go to largest negative number Positive overflows go to +INF
To -INF	Negative overflows go to -INF Positive overflows go to largest positive number

UFL - Underflow. This occurs when a number becomes too small (i.e. too close to zero) to represent properly in the specified precision. If the error is not trapped, the result is affected by the rounding mode as follows:

Nearest	Appropriately signed zero
To zero	Appropriately signed zero
To +INF	Negative underflows go to -0 Positive underflows go to smallest positive number
To -INF	Negative underflows go to smallest negative number Positive underflows go to +0

INX - Inexact. This error occurs whenever a rounded result is obtained which is different from that which would have been calculated if 'infinite' working precision was used. Calculating the sine, cosine or tangent of an angle greater than 10E20 radians causes this error. Also, all OFL errors automatically cause this error, so if the OFL trap is disabled but the INX trap is enabled, an overflow will cause the inexact interrupt to be generated.

System id - These eight bits may be used to determine which type of FPU the system is running. The only one currently defined is bit 31:

bit 31 = 1	implies	hardware FPU
bit 31 = 0	implies	software FPU

The remaining eight bits are reserved by Acorn for further distinction between different FPU types. In the first systems they are all zero.

The FPU control register

The control register is a system dependent entity. It is present to enable programs to, for example, disable a hardware FPU. Its format is dependent on the characteristics of the FPU hardware; as of this writing, it is undefined. Note that the instructions which read and write the control register are privileged. An attempt to access it from a user mode program will cause an error.

B.3 The FPU data processing instructions

There are two classes of FPU data processing instructions, monadic and dyadic. These terms refer to whether the instruction operates on one or two operands respectively. The instruction formats are:

```
MNM{cond}<P>{R}      <dest>,<rhs>
MNM{cond}<P>{R}      <dest>,<lhs>,<rhs>
```

where:
MNM is one of the mnemonics listed below
{cond} is the optional condition
<P> is the required precision, being one of:

S	single precision
D	double precision
E	extended precision

Note that the precision is not optional - it must be given.

{R} is the required rounding mode for the stored result, being one of:

	Round to nearest
P	Round to +INF
M	Round to -INF
Z	Round to zero

This is optional, rounding to nearest being the default if it is omitted.

<dest> is the FPU register to hold the result. The standard names for the FPU registers are F0-F7, and assemblers which recognise the FPU instructions allow other names to be assigned, as for the normal ARM registers.

<lhs> (dyadic only) is the left hand side of the operation. It is an FPU register

<rhs> is the right hand side of a dyadic operation, or the argument of a monadic operation. It is an FPU register, or a small floating point constant. These are the allowed values:

```
0.0     1.0     2.0     3.0
4.0     5.0     0.5     10.0
```

As usual, the immediate operand is preceded by a # sign.

The available dyadic operations are:

```
ADF   add              <dest> = <lhs> + <rhs>
MUF   multiply         <dest> = <lhs> * <rhs>
SUF   subtract         <dest> = <lhs> - <rhs>
RSF   reverse sub.     <dest> = <rhs> - <lhs>
DVF   divide           <dest> = <lhs> / <rhs>
RDF   reverse div.     <dest> = <rhs> / <lhs>
POW   power            <dest> = <lhs> ^ <rhs>
RPW   reverse power    <dest> = <rhs> ^ <lhs>
RMF   remainder        <dest> = <lhs> REM <rhs>
FML   fast multiply    <dest> = <lhs> * <rhs>
FDV   fast divide      <dest> = <lhs> / <rhs>
FRD   fast rev. div.   <dest> = <rhs> / <lhs>
POL   polar angle      <dest> = arctan(<lhs>/<rhs>)
```

Notes:

Reverse power gives a base ten antilog function:

```
        RPWS    F0,F0,#10.0        ;F0 = 10^F0
```

REM <lhs>,<rhs> gives the remainder of the division of **<lhs>** by **<rhs>**. In other words, **a REM b = a-b*n**, where **n** is the nearest integer to **a/b**.

The 'fast' operations **FML, FDV** and **FRD** are performed in single precision, rather than full working precision used for the other calculations. This means that rounding to any precision will always yield a result which is only as accurate as a single precision number.

The **POL** operation is an alternative to the **ATN** operation described below. The two operands may be regarded as the 'opposite' and 'adjacent' lengths (signed) of the angle whose value is required. This function will return a result in the range -PI to +PI radians, whereas the standard **ATN** function only gives a result in the -PI/2 to +PI/2 range.

The monadic operations are:

```
MVF   move             <dest> = <rhs>
MNF   move negated     <dest> = -<rhs>
ABS   absolute value   <dest> = ABS(<dest>)
RND   integer value    <dest> = roundToInteger(<rhs>)
SQT   square root      <dest> = SQR(<rhs>)
LOG   log base 10      <dest> = LOG10(<rhs>)
LGN   log base e       <dest> = LN(<rhs>)
```

```
EXP     e to a power       <dest> = e ^ <rhs>
SIN     sine               <dest> = SIN(<rhs>)
COS     cosine             <dest> = COS(<rhs>)
TAN     tangent            <dest> = TAN(<rhs>)
ASN     arcsine            <dest> = ATN(<rhs>)
ACS     arccosine          <dest> = ACS(<rhs>)
ATN     arctangent         <dest> = ATN(<rhs>)
```

The argument of the **SIN**, **COS** and **TAN** is in radians, and **ASN**, **ACS** and **ATN** return a result in radians. The 'transcendental' functions, from **SQT** onwards, use 'to nearest' rounding for intermediate calculations performed in full working precision, only applying the specified rounding mode as the last operation.

Examples:

```
MUFS    F0,F1,#10.0    ;F0=F1*10, single precision,nearest
POWDZ   F2,F3,F4       ;F2=F3^F4, double precision,zero
SINE    F7,F0          ;F7=SIN(F0), extended, to nearest
EXPE    F0,#1.0        ;F0='e' as an extended constant
```

B.4 The FPU/ARM register transfer instructions

The FPU uses the **FRC/FCR** class of instructions for three purposes: to convert between integer and floating point values, to examine and change the FPU status and control registers, and to perform floating point comparisons.

FIX and **FLT** are the type-conversion instructions. They have the following forms:

```
FIX{cond}<P>{R}   <ARM dest>,<FPU srce>
FLT{cond}<P>{R}   <FPU dest>,<ARM srce>
```

<ARM dest> is R0-R14 (R15 not being useful; see Appendix A)
<ARM srce> is R0-R14 (R15 not being useful)
<FPU dest> is F0-F7
<FPU srce> is F0-F7

The **FIX** operation may result in an **IVO** trap occurring, as explained above.

Examples:

```
FIXNES R0,F2   ;Convert F2 to integer in R0 if NE
FLTSZ  F1,R0   ;Convert R0 to F1, round to zero
```

The instructions to read and write the FPU status register are:

```
RFS{cond}  <ARM  dest>
WFS{cond}  <ARM  srce>
```

<ARM dest> and **<ARM srce>** are the ARM register to or from which the 32-bit FPU status register is transferred. The format of this register is described above. After an **RFS** the ARM register will contain the state of the status flags and interrupt masks. The unused bits will be set to zero, and the system id part will be as described above. A program can clear the flags and set the desired mask bits using **WFS**. Zeros should be placed in the unused bits and the system id bits.

The instructions to read and write the FPU control register are:

```
RFC{cond}  <ARM  dest>
WFC{cond}  <ARM  srce>
```

The format of this register is system dependent. These are privileged instructions and will abort if an attempt is made to execute them in user mode.

Examples:

```
RFS R4
WFC R0
```

The FPU compare instructions have the form:

```
MNM{cond}<P>{R}    <lhs>,<rhs>
```

where all terms are as described in section B.3. The mnemonics are:

```
CMF     compare            <lhs>  -  <rhs>
CNF     compare  negated   <lhs>  +  <rhs>
CMFE    compare            <lhs>  -  <rhs>
CNFE    compare  negated   <lhs>  +  <rhs>
```

The versions with the **E** suffix generate an exception if the operands are 'unordered' (when at least one operand is a NAN) and thus can't be compared. After the instructions, the ARM flags are set as follows:

- **N** set if 'less than' else clear
- **Z** set if 'equal' else clear
- **C** set if 'greater or equal' else clear
- **V** set if 'unordered' else clear

Note that if **V**=1, then **N**=0 and **C**=0.

According to the IEEE standard, when testing for equality or for unorderedness, where the next instruction condition will be **EQ**, **NE**, **VS** or

VC you should use **CMF** (or **CNF**). To test for other relationships (**GT**, **LE** etc.) you should use **CMFE** (or **CNFE**).

Examples:

```
CMFE    F0,#0.0     ;See if F0 is 0.0, extended precision
CMFEE   F1,F2       ;Compare F1, F2 using extended
                    ;precision with disordered exception
CNFS    F3,#1.0     ;Compare single precision F3 with -1
```

B.5 The FPU data transfer instructions

This final group is used to transfer floating point numbers, in the various formats, between main memory and the FPU. The instructions are **LDF** to load a floating point number, and **STF** to store one:

```
LDF{cond}<P>  <FPU dest>,<address>
STF{cond}<P>  <FPU srce>,<address>
```

where:
<P> is as already described, with the additional option of

P packed decimal form

The FPU registers are F0-F7

the **<address>** can take any of the forms described in Appendix A, viz.

<expression> PC-relative offset calculated
[<base>]
[<base>,<offset>]{!}
[<base>],<offset>

where:
<base> is R0-R14
<offset> is **#{+|-}<expression>**
and **{!}** specifies optional write-back.

When a value is stored using **STF**, it is rounded using 'to nearest' rounding to the precision specified in the instruction. (**E** and **P** will always store results without requiring rounding.) If some other rounding method is required, this can be done first using a **MVF** instruction from the register to itself, using the appropriate rounding mode.

If an attempt is made to store a trapping NAN value, an exception will occur if the IVO trap is enabled, otherwise the value will be stored as a non-trapping NAN. OFL errors can occur on stores if the number is too large to be converted to the specified format.

Examples:

```
STFP    F0,[R0]     ;Store F0 in packed format at [R0]
LDFE    F0,pi       ;Load constant from label 'pi'
STFS    F1,[R2],#4  ;Store single prec. number, inc.  R2
```

B.6 Formats of numbers

Each of the four precisions has its own representation of legal numbers and special values. These are described in this section.

Single precision

bit:	31	30——23	22————0		
	Sign	Exponent	msb	Mantissa	lsb

Exponent = eight bits, excess-127
Mantissa = 23 bits, implicit 1. before bit 22

Formats of values

	Sign	Exponent	Mantissa
Non-trapping NAN	x	Maximum	1xxxxxxxxxxxxx...
Trapping NAN	x	Maximum	0<non zero>
INF	s	Maximum	00000000000000...
Zero	s	0	00000000000000...
Denormalised number	s	0	<non zero>
Normalised number	s	Not 0/Max	xxxxxxxxxxxxxx...

where:
x means 'don't care'
s means 1 for negative, 0 for positive (number, zero or INF)
Maximum is 255 (for NANs etc)

Double precision

bit:	31	30——20	19————0		
First Word	Sign	Exponent	msb	Mantissa	lsb
Second Word	msb			mantissa	lsb

Exponent = 11 bits, excess-1023.
Mantissa = 52 bits, implied 1. before bit 19
Formats as above
Maximum exponent (for NANs etc) = 2047

Extended precision

bit:	31	30——16	15——0
First Word	Sign	Exponent	Zeros
Second Word	J		
Third Word	msb	mantissa	lsb

Exponent = 15 bits, excess-16383
Mantissa = 64 bits
Maximum exponent (for NANs etc) = 32767

NB The relative positions of the three parts of the first word had not been finalised as of this writing.

Format of values

	Sign	Exponent	J	Mantissa
Non-trapping NAN	x	Maximum	x	1xxxxxxxxxxxxx...
Trapping NAN	x	Maximum	x	0<non zero>
INF	s	Maximum	0	00000000000000...
Zero	s	0	0	00000000000000...
Denormalised number	s	0	0	<non zero>
Un-normalised numbr	s	Not 0/Max	0	xxxxxxxxxxxxxx...
Normalised number	s	Not 0/Max	1	xxxxxxxxxxxxxx...

Packed decimal

31——0

First Word	Sign	e3	e2	e1	e0	d18	d17	d16
Second Word	d15	d14	d13	d12	d11	d10	d9	d8
Third Word	d7	d6	d5	d4	d3	d2	d1	d0

Each field is four bits
e0-e3 are the exponent digits
d0-d18 are the mantissa digits
Bit 31 of the first word is the sign of the number
Bit 30 of the first word is the sign of the exponent

Format of values

	bit 31	30	e3-e0	d18-d0
Non-trapping NAN	x	x	&FFFF	d18>7, rest non 0
Trapping NAN	x	x	&FFFF	d18<=7, rest non 0
INF	s	x	&FFFF	&00000000000000...
Zero	0	0	&0000	&00000000000000...
Number	s	s	&0000-&9999	&1-&99999999999...

Note that when -0 is stored in this format it is converted to +0.

Appendix C
Instruction set

Data Processing

31–28	27–26	25	24–21	20	19–16	15–12	11–0
Cond	00	I	OpCode	S	Rn	Rd	Operand 2

Cond: Condition field

0000	EQ (EQual)
0001	NE (NEver)
0010	CS (Carry Set)
0011	CC (Carry Clear)
0100	MI (MInus)
0101	PL (PLus)
0110	VS (oVerflow Set)
0111	VC (oVerflow Clear)
1000	HI (HIgher)
1001	LS (Lower or Same)
1010	GE (Greater or Equal)
1011	LT (Less Than)
1100	GT (Greater Than)
1101	LE (Less than or Equal)
1110	AL (ALways)
1111	NV (NeVer)

OpCode: Operation code

0000	AND
0001	EOR
0010	SUB
0011	RSB
0100	ADD
0101	ADC
0110	SBC
0111	RSC
1000	TST
1001	TEQ
1010	CMP
1011	CMN
1100	ORR
1101	MOV
1110	BIC
1111	MVN

I: Immediate operand bit. This defines exactly what Operand 2 is. If the I bit is 0, Operand 2 is a register, with the register number held in bits 0 to 3 and the shift applied to that register in bits 4 to 11. If the I bit is 1, Operand 2 is an immediate value, with bits 0 to 7 holding the 8 bit value, and bits 8 to 11 holding the shift applied to that value.

S: Set condition codes. If this bit is set to 0, the condition codes are not altered after the instruction has executed. If it is set to 1, they are altered.

Rn: First operand register.

Rd: Destination register.

31–28	27–25	24	23–0
Cond	101	L	Offset

Branch and Branch with link

L: Link bit. 0=Branch, 1=Branch with link

31–28	27–22	21	20	19–16	15–12	11–8	7–4	3–0
Cond	000000	A	S	Rn	Rd	Rs	1001	Rm

Multiply and multiply-accumulate

A: Accumulate bit. 0=multiply, 1=multiply with accumulate

Single Data transfer

31 28	27 26	25	24	23	22	21	20	19 16	15 12	11 0
Cond	01	I	P	U	B	W	L	Rn	Rd	Offset

P: Pre/Post indexing. 0=post (offset added after transfer). 1=pre (offset added before transfer).
U: Up/Down bit. 0=down (Offset subtracted from base). 1=Up (Offset added to base).
B: Byte/Word bit. 0=transfer word, 1=transfer byte.
W: Write-back. 0=No write back, 1=Write address into base.

Block data transfer

31 28	27 25	24	23	22	21	20	19 16	15 0
Cond	100	P	U	S	W	L	Rn	Register list

S: PSR & Force user mode. 0=do not load PSR or force user mode. 1=load PSR or force user mode.

Software Interrupt

31 28	27 24	23 0
Cond	1111	Comment field (ignored by ARM)

Co-processor data operations

31 28	27 24	23 20	19 16	15 12	11 8	7 5	4	3 0
Cond	1110	CP Opc	CRn	CRd	CP#	CP	0	CRm

CP Opc: Co-processor operation code. **CRn:** Co-processor operand register. **CRd:** Co-processor destination register. **CP#:** Co-processor number. **CP:** Co-processor information

Co-processor data transfers

31 28	27 25	24	23	22	21	20	19 16	15 12	11 8	7 0
Cond	110	P	U	N	W	L	Rn	CRd	CP#	Offset

N: Transfer Length.

Co-processor register transfers

31 28	27 24	23 21	20	19 16	15 12	11 8	7 5	4	3 0
Cond	1110	CP Opc	L	CRn	Rd	CP#	CP	1	CRm

L: Load/Store bit. 0=Store to co-processor, 1=Load from co-processor.

Undefined instructions.

31 28	27 24	23 8	7 4	3 0
Cond	0001	xxxxxxxxxxxxxxxx	1xx1	xxxx

31 28	27 25	24 5	4	3 0
Cond	011	xxxxxxxxxxxxxxxxxxxx	1	xxxx

Index